HI-Q
CHRISTIANS

HI-Q CHRISTIANS

A Practical Guide on
How to be a
High Quality Christian

BY
ORAL
WITHROW

Vision 2 Grow
and
Warner Press, Inc.
Anderson, Indiana

Copyright ©1993 by Warner Press, Inc.
ISBN #0-87162-657-8   Stock #D4050
All rights reserved.
Printed in the United States of America
Warner Press, Inc.

David C. Shultz, Editor in Chief
Dan Harman, Book Editor
Cover by Larry Lawson

Contents

Foreword

"Total Quality" has swept worldwide manufacturing and management. Gone are the years when consumers tolerated unsafe cars, appliances that won't work, or service departments that can't repair what is broken. We expect the quality to be thorough when we buy a new automobile—not just an engine that starts, but trim that fits, a radio that works, paint that is smooth, and tires capable of surviving potholes.

Quality control managers pursue a "zero defect" standard even though it is impossible. To expect less is to tolerate heart pacemakers that work ninety percent of the time. Ninety percent just isn't good enough when it's your heart.

This quest for total quality has raised standards worldwide. In many industries service is vastly improved. Telephones almost always connect. Major surgery is far less risky. Millions of air miles are traveled with seldom a crash. Most new cars have a life-expectancy far greater than one hundred thousand miles.

Quality may be new to business but not to Christianity. Since Christians are patterned after Jesus Christ, "total quality" takes on a supernatural standard. We are to be just like Jesus. The quality is not limited to Sundays or to the sacred. It totally includes both sacred and secular all seven days of every week. Every part of us is to be thoroughly Christian—relationships, attitudes, prayer, behavior.

True, many immediately insist that the quality of Christ is an impossible "zero defect" standard. Yet, dare we settle in advance for anything less?

Leith Anderson
Pastor: Wooddale Church, Eden Prarie, MN
Author: *A Church for the 21st Century*

Introduction

Many church groups have inaugurated programs to increase attendance and membership in the decade of the nineties. Increased participation is anticipated to be a prelude to a wider and more effective ministry for God's church at the beginning of the next century.

Numerical growth is desirable but it is not enough. Unfortunately, if the church produces more of the type of Christians it has often produced in the twentieth century, the world, and the church itself, will not benefit greatly.

Hi-Q Christians—high quality Christians—are needed. High quality Christians are persons who make a difference in the community, in the church, and in the family as well as in the fabric of their own lives.

At least four characteristics will find obvious expression in the life of a high quality Christian: *humility, generosity, accountability,* and *maturity.*

This book is intended for a general Christian audience, for personal study, and for group study. Each chapter invites the participation of you, the reader, with questions and discussion guides provided at the end of each chapter. Side-bars highlight relevant quotes and additional illustrations and stimulate further thought. Many of the stories are taken from the lives of high quality Christians I have known—common people just like you and me who are attempting to grow in their faith.

How to Use with Small Groups
Or in a Sunday School Class

Many small groups meet weekly for fellowship, prayer, mutual support, and study. They may take eight or nine weeks to read about and discuss a subject. Sunday school classes and other small groups may prefer to use material for a quarter of the year—thirteen weeks.

Groups who prefer an eight- or nine-week study will find information at the end of each chapter that will help stimulate discussion. These statements and questions may be duplicated.

Groups who prefer a thirteen-week schedule for considering high-quality Christianity and high-commitment churches may use the following guide. Adaptations may be made, obviously, for a shorter term.

First meeting: Introductory Session (see Appendix) and distribution of the book *Hi-Q Christians.*

Second through *tenth* meetings: Discussion of questions at the end of chapters one through nine in *Hi-Q Christians.*

Eleventh and *twelfth* meetings: An Appendix provides a guide for the eleventh session and two options for the twelfth. Statements and questions may be copied for each member of the group.

Thirteenth meeting: A guide for suggesting a plan for renewal in your local congregation. See "Concluding Session: Toward Renewal" in the Appendix.

4

1

Hi-Q: Quality Christianity

qual-i-ty,... any character or characteristic which may
make an object good or bad, commendable or reprehen-
sible; the degree of excellence which a thing possesses;...
superiority; excellence; as, a person of quality. (*Webster's*
28).

"My Most Unforgettable Sunday School Teacher" was the
writing assignment I had from the editor.

Immediately I thought of two men. The first was Lovell
Lanham who taught our Intermediate Boys Class, which today
would be called the junior high class and would be coeduca-
tional. The educational process and the small, crowded, base-
ment classroom setting were not the most effective for learning. Lovell, a factory worker, stood in front of us with an open
lesson manual and tried in vain to get us to participate in dis-
cussions. I'll always remember our class had parties that
included a lot of food. We played softball in the summer and
basketball in the winter. Still unforgettable to me was Lovell's
concern and thoughtful words to each of us. Lovell was also
the song leader for our worship services. He remains unforgettable: he touched my shoulder with affection and understanding during a time when I needed encouragement, and he con-

tinued to inquire of me long after I had left my home town to attend college.

The second person who came to mind is Ray Stewart, the boys' church league basketball coach. Many of us were very limited in athletic ability; dribbling a basketball one time down the court consumed our week's allowance of coordination skills. Ray liked to win games but he also had the ability to instill in boys a respect and love for Christ. He was in the steel business and came directly from work to coach our boy's basketball and softball teams. His voice was deep and gravelly but his spirit was bright and generous. Unforgettable.

Lovell and Ray were typical of several persons whom I met when I started going to church as a thirteen-year-old. These two were high quality Christians. They attended worship services regularly, they prayed for people to be saved, and while they lived a different life-style from most persons, they made a difference in the lives of many of us. Lovell and Ray were to go through major tests of their faith a few years later but they were true to Christ and their own discipleship.

CHRISTIANITY THAT MAKES NO DIFFERENCE

Christians like Lovell and Ray are a blessing to any community and any church. Many persons, however, who claim Christ do not exhibit the same quality these and other persons have demonstrated.

Nominal Christianity is not that impressive. Nominal means a person is counted as a Christian but is not serious about the implications for his or her life.

Popular Christianity is just that, popular—a level of commitment practiced by a church-going population but not meaningful to either churchgoers or persons outside the church.

Dead Christianity has many expressions and needs no explanation; it is lifeless.

Sick Christianity, characterized by neurotic or psychotic behavior, is evidenced daily on television and in the life of nearly every congregation. Author Stephen Arterburn says,

"Faith becomes toxic when individuals use God or religion for profit, power, pleasure and/or prestige" (1991, 28).

Doucette speaks of the sick expression of the faith: "Egos, desire for power, searching for a quick fix for pain and the need to manipulate have produced a generation of faithful followers whose faith is toxic" (1991, page x).

Nominal, popular, dead, sick—these and other negative words are used to describe the blasé life of many Christians in our culture. What hurts the earnest follower of Christ is that the descriptions are often true. Neither the passive nor the hyperactive Christianity experienced by many people is fulfilling or satisfying.

HIGH QUALITY CHRISTIANS

A different type of Christian does exist. As you read some of the following descriptions you may say, "Oh yes, I know some persons who live like that." It can be observed that

• some people are living the Christian faith remarkably in keeping with the patterns stated in the New Testament.
• some people do appear to seek first the kingdom of God in all they say and do.
• some have about them an aura of joy in both difficult and rewarding circumstances.
• some are operating on a different wave-length from the rest of the world.

These persons have been spoken of as high commitment Christians by Lyle Schaller. The persons in this group are not odd individuals, but they *are* different. They take their faith seriously and their faith enables them to enjoy life more than others seem to do. (The distinctiveness is expressed in the King James Version of Titus 2:14 and 1 Peter 2:9 as "a peculiar people." It may be just as strong in a later translation, "a people of his own," as in the New Revised Standard Version.)

7

> *So it is with the credo of so many of today's church attenders: "You go to the meetings and serve on the boards and committees, you grapple with the issues and do the work of the church and pay the bills—and I'll come along for the ride. But if things do not suit me, I'll criticize and complain and probably bail out—my thumb is always out for a better ride."*
> —R. Ken Hughes (1992, 38)

Dan Rather, anchor of CBS Evening News, was reared in a Southern Baptist home in Texas. He confesses, "Religion, especially prayer, has been an intimate personal companion at my side in my everyday routine ever since the earliest mists of my childhood" (Rather and Wyden 204, 1991). His wife Jean is a Lutheran and they have reared their children primarily in that Christian tradition. In his autobiography, I *Remember,* Rather candidly states a difference in the discipleship he has seen and what he is experiencing:

> Frankly, our faith is not as rock solid, not as well founded as that of our fathers and mothers, and their fathers and mothers. We must face the unpleasant fact that because we have an easier life and more of life's riches we're inclined to become soft and flabby spiritually, and especially in the religious sense. The trials of the Great Depression are long gone. So is our great war, World War II, which we could have lost to demons who were real threats to conquer our homeland. A lack of fear in day-to-day living can lead to malaise of the soul; maybe that has happened to us (209).

Rather speaks for many persons who see a difference between high quality Christian living and the popular, less demanding, religious life-style often associated with church membership. George Gallup, Jr., says that ten percent of Americans are deeply committed Christians. "These people are a breed apart," Gallup observes. "They are more tolerant of people of diverse backgrounds. They are more involved in practical Christianity. They are absolutely committed to prayer," and "far, far happier than the rest of the population" (1991).

Our concern is not with a minimal saving grace required to get one into heaven. God has provided that grace and it is only by grace that anyone is saved. God accepts our imperfections better than we do, and persons about whom we may have had serious doubts will inherit eternal life. On the other hand, they may be somewhat surprised to learn you and I also made it through.

A life-style intentionally based on the teachings and spirit of Jesus is needed in the nineties. That life-style is something

---

The Christian with a high quality practice of the faith gives evidence that he or she
- *is living close to God*
- *loves people*
- *looks forward to worship with other Christians*
- *has a sense of vocation either in a daily job or in volunteer responsibilities*
- *utilizes resources with an awareness of divine guidance*
- *has a hope beyond death*
- *brings personal strength to many other persons, both Christians and those who are not Christian.*

each follower of Christ may choose, ignore, occasionally refer to, or even reject. Discipleship encompasses more than being saved from hell. It is a life patterned on the example and teachings of Jesus.

What is it about these persons—these high quality Christians—and their practice of the faith that sets them apart from passive, popular, neurotic Christians? What are the attitudes and behavioral patterns we see in these people who are worthy of emulation?

I will attempt to answer that question, but not without letting you know that I do so with a great deal of hesitance. I have pastored many high quality Christians. Each was unique, not a recognizable copy of any other high quality Christian, though not dissimilar either. I have friends who I believe live as close to Jesus' teachings as is humanly possible. They are persons with diverse personality types, relational skills, and leadership gifts; they use a variety of words to speak of their religious experiences.

They are not all from stable Christian homes, though that heritage seems to be more common. These high commitment Christians are not necessarily old. Some are young; as they grow older the quality of their life-style improves.

The high quality Christians I have known invariably had some personal weakness. In most it was not a moral or sinful weakness but a personality trait which they would have preferred to overcome but never did. For example, one person, though patient with all acquaintances and fellow workers, seemed repeatedly to be impatient with his family. On the job and in church meetings he was known as a very kind and thoughtful man, but his son knew him as a critic; the man loved his son but his son seemed never to do a project in a way pleasing to his dad. The man eventually realized his weakness and made apologies. This exemplary Christian grieved over the pain he caused his son.

High quality Christians keep wanting to grow. They pray for and they work for growth. One high quality Christian I knew for many years was my wife's grandmother. Her family and community speak of her positive attitudes, rich faith, and exemplary life. Though she and her husband Shum were dirt farmers, their children all became professionals—educators, pastors, civil servants. One of grandmother's legs was crippled from a childhood accident but she managed a large household with a minimum of funds. She encouraged her children to develop a personal faith. Her optimism and patience were a source of encouragement both for her family and the community. When she was ninety-two years old Laura and I were visiting in her home near Philadelphia, Mississippi. Grandmother and I were talking that day and she said quite seriously, "Oral, I want you to pray for me. I need to be more humble."

Without exception, I believe each of these Christians is aware that he or she is living a high commitment life and is enjoying a richness in life not experienced by most other persons. Without exception, however, I believe these persons would be embarrassed to know that I or anyone else classified them as exemplars of the Christian faith.

The Apostle Paul is an example of a person who knew his limitations. Paul also knew that his commitment to Christ was significant and his practice of the faith was exemplary (1 Corinthians 4:16 and 11:1).

Hi-Q CHRISTIANS, A GOAL OF THE CHURCH

Hi-Q Christians are not a rare breed. Many are active in their churches. Even so, many more Christians are living lives that are less than challenging. It is crucial that the church so structure its evangelism and nurturing ministries that high quality Christians are an anticipated, rather than chance, result.

High quality Christians will make a difference
- in the community
- in the home
- in the school
- in the workplace
- in the daily experience of their own lives

Our Savior makes the distinct contrast in his words:

> *The spiritual life is a gift. It is the gift of the Holy Spirit, who lifts us up into the kingdom of God's love. But to say that being lifted up into the kingdom of love is a divine gift does not mean that we wait passively until the gift is offered to us. Jesus tells us to set our hearts on the kingdom. Setting our hearts on something involves not only serious aspiration but also strong determination. A spiritual life requires human effort.*
>
> —Henri J. M. Nouwen (1981, 65)

Therefore, whoever breaks one of the least of these commandments, and teaches others to do the same, will be called least in the kingdom of heaven; but whoever does them and teaches them will be called great in the kingdom of heaven. For I tell you, unless your righteousness exceeds that of the Pharisees, you will never enter the kingdom of heaven. —Matthew 5:19-20

If the church focuses only on numerical increase, but fails to proclaim a discipleship that is Christlike, then Christians will fall short of the Bible's requirement that we be the yeast or the light or the salt in the society in which we find ourselves.

Production is a mechanistic word but I will use it temporarily. If the production of high quality Christians is not at least one goal of the church, then we have a recurring problem. Carl F. George suggests the problem: "Churches find that each time they grow a little, their quality lessens, so they must scramble to implement a new organizational system geared to their current size." He adds, "Almost every growing church I've encountered faces insurmountable limits on its ability to expand its structure without serious disruption of quality" (1991, 42-43).

George Gallup, Jr., says most American Christians do not know basic Christian teachings and are not significantly different from non-Christians in their life-style. The church can surely do a better job of producing quality Christians than Gallup's analysis would indicate.

What is suggested is not a tool by which we measure spirituality or churchmanship—another form of legalism. Christians come in all shapes and sizes, and each person is at one of many stages of faith development.

Whatever the stage of faith development, is it not appropriate to expect a quality of life in keeping with the pattern taught by Jesus? Maturity is also a characteristic of Christians at all levels of the Christian pilgrimage. Maturity, in a broader sense, is intentionally learning from Jesus and intentionally practicing what Jesus taught. Quality Christian living can be reasonably expected from all who claim Christ as Savior; increasing maturity can be expected from all disciples.

HUMBLE, GENEROUS, ACCOUNTABLE, MATURE

In August 1991, I said to George Barna, following one of his lectures on the future of the church, "You have spoken about high quality churches. What is the quality of the Christians these churches will produce? What do your studies indicate are the characteristics of quality Christian living?" He surprised me when he responded, "I don't know. We haven't studied that at all."

With a keen awareness of my limitations in doing so, I exercise some boldness in suggesting that the church needs to set forth a standard of excellence and guide an increasing number of believers into what we will call in this writing a Hi-Q Christian experience and witness.

Hi-Q Christians are essential to the church's life and ministry for the twenty-first century. Christians who live with the same values and same styles as non-Christians will not be initiators of change in a nation and world that badly need change. A primary task of the church is to guide Christians

> *Faith is more than doctrine, belief, religious law, or creed. It is more than something we receive from God, or learn in a confirmation class, or profess in a Bar Mitzvah ceremony. Faith is always process.*
> *Faith is movement.*
>
> —Kenneth Stokes (1990, 5)

into a faith that makes a difference, not a faith that is an option or department of their lives.

Though there are other foundations of a dynamic faith, four will be identified. These four characteristics are essential if our lives as Christians are to make any difference. The Hi-Q Christian is humble, generous, accountable, mature. Discover with me the difference the experiences suggested by these four words can mean.

Editor's Note:

The following section, "For Meditation and Discussion," is presented in this chapter and throughout the book on facing pages to enable photo-copying to be more easily done.

FOR MEDITATION OR DISCUSSION

1. Identify by name four persons you consider to be high quality Christians:

_____

_____

_____

_____

2. What was/is it about the lives of these persons that made them distinctively Christian?

3. How do you define spirituality?

4. What disciplines enable and enhance the spiritual dimension of a person's life?

5. In what ways do high-quality Christians make a difference:
- in the community?
- in the home?
- in school?
- in the workplace?
- in their own daily experience of life?

6. Compare the differences in the life-styles of
- a nominal Christian
- a high quality Christian
- a person who is not a Christian
- a church member

7. In what way does your local church challenge and inspire members to a high-quality Christian life?

8. What training does your local church provide that helps persons grow as Christians?

9. How do you define Christian maturity?

10. What kinds of worship experiences encourage you in your spiritual pilgrimage?

11. What word most nearly begins to describe your present life as a Christian?
- healthy
- stalled
- sick
- some other word:
- nominal
- discouraged
- searching
- mature
- exciting
- beginning

2

Have You Tried Being Humble Lately?

O come, let us sing to the LORD;
    let us make a joyful noise the rock of our salvation!
Let us come into his presence with thanksgiving;
    let us make a joyful noise to him with songs of praise!
For the Lord is a great God,
    and a great King above all gods.
In his hand are the depths of the earth;
    the heights of the mountains are his also.
The sea is his, for he made it,
    and the dry land, which his hands have formed.
O come, let us worship and bow down,
    let us kneel before the Lord, our Maker!
For he is our God,
    and we are the people of his pasture,
    and the sheep of his hand   (Psalm 95:1-7).

Hi-Q Christians are humble. Their lives result in
- humble attitudes
- humble actions
- humble conversation
- humble life-styles

The word *humble* may mean very different things to different people. I am not suggesting that humble people always

> *Humility does not rest, in final count, upon bafflement and discouragement and self-disgust at our shabby lives, a browbeaten, dog-slinking attitude. It rests upon the disclosure of the consummate wonder of God, upon finding that only God counts, that all our own self-originated intentions are works of straw.*
> —Thomas Kelly (*A Testament of Devotion* 62)

let others have their way. Humble people may not smile all the time. Humble people may not display a self-effacing attitude or make self-degrading remarks.

The Hi-Q Christian may be shy or outgoing, an introvert or extrovert, a dominant person or one whom others often fail to notice. Whatever the person's traits, humility is a part of his or her life. A high quality Christian does not call attention to himself or herself but may command attention; power or position are not sought though it is often realized. A great deal of time or energy is not spent fretting over the economical or vocational advantages of other persons.

Humility, as the Bible teaches it, centers on two relationships:

1. Reverence for God.
2. Respect for persons.

In this chapter the focus is on reverence for God. Respect for persons is the subject of the next chapter.

GOD IS A PERSON

God is a person, and we reverence him by knowing God as a person. In our Christian tradition we speak of our God as being a living God. We believe that gods that can be placed on a shelf, housed in a public shelter, or carried around on a

> *Instead of supernatural, I prefer the phrase above nature.*
>
> *And if God is above nature, he is above my feelings. His involvement in my life is supernatural. I live in a natural realm, empowered by the transcendent God, whether I happen to feel that transcendence or not.*
>
> —John Huffman (1991, 15)

chain are humanly made gods and not worthy of worship. Jesus insisted that "God is a spirit" (alive, being, personal) rather than a material object in a holy place (John 4:16-26). However, we have at times attempted to reduce God to a manageable size. We sometimes

• use God or God's name as a *good luck piece,* when we want to win a contest or desire a special benefit, such as when baseball players cross themselves for good luck before going to bat;

• use God as a helper in a *time of weakness* and act as if God is not necessary when we are physically, financially, and relationally comfortable, for example faithfully worshiping during an illness or crisis with a child but seldom worshiping when the child is out of danger;

• use God as a source of *personal fulfillment,* someone to provide our wants or enable us to meet our goals, an overall answer for the help-wanted section of our lives, as in praying for help to pass a test in a college course;

• use God for our *special days*—Christmas, Easter, when we get married, when we dedicate our children, and when we are buried.

When we use God as a resource for our purposes and our goals, then we do not live humbly.

During my college days I often received an invitation to visit with the dean. He may have wanted to speak with me about improving my grades. The dean may have wanted to inform me that he had learned how many hours I was working and that I would have to reduce my hours of employment. He may have wanted to talk with me about the door on my room that had been knocked off the hinges.

I came to know the dean as someone whom I had to satisfy and as one who enforced the rules for students. He was a rather large man, had a round face, and wore glasses—giving him an owlish look. To me he was Mr. Rules, Mr. Privilege (if I were to have any), and one who could give me permission to do what I wanted to do or limit my privileges.

In my senior and subsequent years I learned more about this stern, owlish-looking fellow. He was one of the most involved Christians in our community with persons who were denied political and economic benefits. He traveled every weekend to pastor a church a 120 miles distant and was loved by his congregation. He was most interested in me and what my plans were. He was courageous, disciplined, loving, visionary, and thoughtful—a wonderful person. I was humbled as I came to know Dean Russell Olt as a person.

Reverence for God means we come to know him as a person. As long as we see God as a watch dog or as an outdated old man then we cannot revere him and certainly we will not live humbly.

Jesus said God is a Spirit. *Spirit* does not refer to a mist. As humans, we know that we are more than our physical bodies or even our intelligence; we are a spirit. Our spirit is our real self, our very soul. So is God a spirit, and when we reverence God as a person—as one who cares and loves, who can be hurt, is generous and ultimately concerned about us—then we begin to be reverent. We are humbled that such a great person can be involved with us. We cannot be arrogant when we personally relate to the great God of the universe.

WAYS WE REVERENCE GOD

Praise is a way we reverence God, and praise keeps us humble. Praise is more than a casual thank you or an informal

> *Worship is an active response to God whereby we declare His worth ... not passive but participative ... not simply a mood; it is a response ... not just a feeling; it is a declaration ... not primarily a state of the art but rather a state of the heart ... [that is] the driving desire behind the worship life of the believer.*
> —Ronald Allen and Gordon Borror (1982, 16-23)

acknowledgment that God may have had something to do with the events of last week.

The author of Hebrews thought it absolutely essential for Christians to get together with other Christians each week for worship (Heb. 10:25). Praise is not an option for the Christian; it is central to the Christian experience and to the whole of Christian faith.

Though sometimes a private practice, open and public praise underscores a person's and a family's dependence on God. We thank God for flowers, for trees of the field, for food, for healing, for life itself. Praise proclaims that whatever happens, we are God's people and he is our God. In response to all that God has done, humble persons worship; they set apart special and regular times for praise, prayer, and the focusing of life, or, as the Quakers have said it, "centering down."

Corporate worship, worship each week with a group of Christians, is a priority for the Hi-Q Christian. Other interests and activities fit in around worship with the body of Christ, the church. In Sunday worship we express reliance on God, an interdependence with the fellowship of believers. During corporate worship we meet in a special way, a way not duplicated in any other setting or relationship. The humble insist they are incapable of living without mutual thanks and supplication to God in the company of believers.

During personal moments my wife likes to hear me say, "I love you." She also appreciates courtesies and other public acknowledgments that I honor her as my wife, as a responsible and talented person. Similarly, we revere God by thanking and honoring him publicly for who he is and what he has done in our lives.

Personal and private worship are also part of the life of humility. Hi-Q Christians find time for Bible reading, quiet meditation, and communion (prayer) with God. Some call these times private devotions. These Christians have many other daily experiences of communion with God, in times of decision or trouble. Occasionally, these persons have an euphoric realization of the presence of the Divine, for no apparent reason and with no discernible cause.

Probably no other aspect of the Christian life is so personal and subjective. Probably no aspect of the Christian life has been more the object of legalism. The absence of a prayer discipline has caused a great sense of guilt and frustration for even deeply committed Christians. The practice of personal and private worship has been a problem for many Christians and has been a formidable barrier to many new Christians. Perhaps a part of the problem can be identified.

One study in the 1980s reported that most Christians prayed little more than three minutes a day; pastors prayed about seven. Most Christians agree that amount of time seems

> *I've experienced God's presence most powerfully in worship situations, often during the singing, I suppose because when we sing to him, we are looking hard in his direction.*
>
> *I have also experienced God's presence vividly under the preaching and praying of Spirit-filled men [and women] of God. Singing, praying, and preaching are basic channels for corporate realization of his holy presence.*
>
> —J. I. Packer (1991, 18-19)

woefully short for private devotions, however, the inference is dangerous. One can conclude that if Christians would spend more time in private devotions they would be more Christlike. More minutes, it would seem, make us more spiritual.

When we uncritically accept this statistic we may believe that prayers or personal devotion times can be evaluated on the basis of how closely they follow a designated pattern of praise, thanks, petition, and intercession. Thus, private worship becomes a specific prescription of thoughts and activities and is valued on the basis of time spent; using these standards, we judge our spiritual lives in unfair ways.

The truth is that many Hi-Q Christians insist that though they spend some time in Bible reading and personal prayer at the beginning or end of the day, significant times of worship are experienced throughout the day. These experiences are often serendipitous as Christians intentionally remain open to praise and prayer.

"Prayer is the single most significant thing that will help turn inner turmoil into peace. Prayer is the Answer." That is what Charles Swindoll says. He asks, then, why prayer is a struggle, making so many of us feel guilty, dissatisfied and "unhappy with our prayer life." Swindoll thinks that we have erred in our identification of what real prayer or personal devotions are. In particular he says we err in trying to equate prayer's meaning to the number of hours spent doing it.

Swindoll observes that spiritual giants like Dietrich Bonhoeffer, Martin Luther, E. M. Bounds, Alexander Maclaren, Samuel Rutherford, Hudson Taylor, John Henry Jowett, G. Campbell Morgan, Joseph Parker, Charles Haddon Spurgeon, F. F. Meyer, A. W. Tozer, H. A. Ironside, V. Raymond Edman, and William Culbertson are ones who taught about prayer and labored at it but expressed dissatisfaction with the extent of their prayer life. It would seem that if the amount of hours spent in prayer were in direct correspondence to its effectiveness then these persons would certainly be satisfied (1982, 146-149).

Instead of prayer being joyful, abundant, and something to be anticipated, for many Christians private prayer continues to produce guilt because one can never pray enough. Of course, one can go the route of the persons who isolate themselves from society and spend numerous hours each day in prayer, but this causes problems for those who have many vocational, family, and mundane tasks for which they are responsible. Besides, even persons who have given hours, maybe five or six a day, to private devotions, do not always appear to escape an urge to spend even more time in prayer. Could that not be more neurotic than spiritual?

It is difficult to find lengthy prayer times in the life of Jesus; we only assume that he prayed all night in Gethsemane. The record would indicate he had several periods of prayer that night, and certainly it was an extreme circumstance.

We find evidence in the scriptures that Jesus went apart from his followers and the crowd on occasion for a time of personal refreshment. Also, the gospel record indicates Jesus lived with a continuous awareness of God's presence, like the type of life we have already indicated. Even so, the greatest prayer, one that is the model given by Jesus himself, can be prayed in less than thirty seconds.

The Hi-Q Christian's prayer life is characterized more by a continuous attitude of prayer, communion with God, than it is by isolated and legalistically defined hours alone. The Hi-Q Christian does regularly find time for regular personal, private worship, however.

There is a way of ordering our mental life on more than one level at once. On one level we may be thinking, discussing, seeing, calculating, meeting all the demands of external affairs. But deep within, behind the scenes, at a profounder level, we may also be in prayer and adoration, song and worship and a gentle receptiveness to divine breathings.
—Thomas Kelly (*A Testament of Devotion*, 35)

CONFESSION

Confession is another way we reverence God, and it is humbling.
The following experience does not fit readily into some of our traditional ideas on salvation and holiness; I am aware of that. On New Year's Eve we had a come-and-go communion service at Park Place Church. My wife and I arrived and took a place near the front of the sanctuary. We picked up a sheet of paper with devotional thoughts, scripture references, and instructions about how to go forward to receive the bread and the cup. We spent some time in meditation and then bowed at the altar and our pastors served us. I started to pray. The only prayer I prayed was, "Lord forgive me of my sins."

I do not believe that everyone commits a sin every day. I believe the Lord saves us from our sins, but I needed a time to confess to God that some of my actions the past year were not right. A touch of bitterness had become lodged in my heart. I was jealous of some friends who were financially better off than I. I had been impatient and thoughtless with some persons who are very dear to me. I needed to confess and I poured out all of my personal malice into one confession.

Confession is reverence for God. God does not make us acknowledge guilt or promise to behave. When we do so, then we honor him as one who has created us and has our best interest at heart.

Confession is an act of humility. We are prone to words and acts that cover up our sins, our cruelty, our negligence, our hard heartedness. When we confess to God, the very act humbles us. Our pride is forced aside by the confession.

DIVINE DIRECTION

Divine direction is evidence of reverence and humility.
The Old Testament writer told us to acknowledge God in all our ways and God will direct our paths. The New Testament writer encouraged us to say, "If the Lord wills, we shall live

and we shall do this or that tomorrow" (James 4:13-15).

A few years ago I was in a home when the son and new daughter-in-law of the family stopped to visit. They wanted to talk to dad and mom about the opportunity they had to buy a home. Was it a good deal? Could they afford it? Was it really the best time to buy? They were honoring their parents' experience by sitting with them and talking about a decision. The parents, wisely, did not make the decision for them. They did, however, point out some dangers and some opportunities and assured the young couple they were standing by to love and to help, whatever choice they made. We demonstrate appreciation and humility when we seek counsel and guidance.

We have often perceived God as someone who wants to force us to do something we do not want to do and who will see that we receive severe punishment if we do not follow instructions explicitly. Divine direction is not a form of playing checkers where each move is dictated by a Divine Expert. Divine direction comes from consistently and repeatedly conversing with God about the meaning and purpose of life and how best to live it to its fullest. Seeking God's counsel is a reverent act; you do not have to do it. It is an humbling act that enriches your life in a way most persons never experience.

An enormous sense of meaning and fulfillment can come to life when one can say, "The Lord guided me into this opportunity for service, but he let me make the choice."

GRACE

The acceptance of grace is a humble act. Our world, our nation, and the church need persons who have been humbled by the acceptance of God's grace.

Years ago Southern Baptist Pastor Roy Angel told the story of a young man who began drinking and living a wild life. The youth lived at home with his parents, and his life-style was an embarrassment to them. Late at night he would stagger in, drunk, dirty, and foul smelling. His mother would get up from her bed and guide him to his bed and he would pass

27

out. She would tenderly hold him in her arms and kiss his forehead. Her friends learned of her actions and asked her, "Why do you do this?" Her simple reply was, "It is the only time he will let me love him."

God's grace is like that. Whatever we have done, he loves us and is waiting for opportunities to express his affection and concern for us.

It is humbling to know that God loves us even when we forget him, week after week. God loves us even though we have not honored his name. God loves us when we have treated his other children with disrespect. God loves us when we have chosen to disregard the teachings of his Son Jesus Christ. God loves each of us, whatever we have been or done. That is humbling.

Humility is an enriching and rewarding experience. Humility is attractive in the life of the disciple of Jesus.

FOR MEDITATION OR DISCUSSION

1. God is a person! Not a thing! That being so, what does it indicate about how you relate to God?

2. What expressions of praise are meaningful and satisfying to you?

3. What words from worship leaders, experiences, or settings best call you to worship?
- a scripture reading
- a hymn, or choral music
- silent meditation
- organ music
- friendly greeting
- architecture
- exuberant singing
- a poem
- other

4. Check either *a* or *b*, then any other items under each.
(a) _____ I have a time of private worship regularly.
I read the scriptures _____
I pray _____
I spend time just thinking, meditating _____
I also _____

(b) _____ I find it difficult to have a time of personal devotion because
I do not enjoy reading scriptures _____
I do not know how to word my prayers _____
When I meditate my mind just wanders. It is difficult for me to confess _____

I tend to fall asleep _____
When I ask God for something I just do not believe it will
    happen _____
I do not ask for help easily _____
Other:

5. What decisions do you pray about, seeking divine guidance?

What decisions do you make yourself, believing God has-
    given you a mind and experience that qualifies you to
    make those decisions?

6. Do you have difficulty accepting God's forgiveness?

Do you understand why?

What counsel do you need to help you accept forgiveness
    from God and forgive yourself?

3

Respect For Persons

The humble person not only reverences God; the humble person also respects others. The vertical relationship with God is at the core of our discipleship. Repeatedly, however, the New Testament insists that the horizontal relationship with people is integral to our relationship with God. Jesus summarized it pointedly

> "You shall love the Lord your God with all your heart, and with all your soul, and with all your mind." This is the greatest and first commandment. And the second is like it: "You shall love your neighbor as yourself." On these two commandments hang all the law and the prophets (Matt. 22:37-40).

This teaching of Jesus is explicit, though we may read it as abstract theology or philosophy. It is an ideal, but Jesus' summary of the commandments is also practical. On another occasion he taught his disciples to include in their prayer the phrase "forgive us our debts, as we also have forgiven our debtors." Lest they miss the point, he gave a precise interpretation:

> For if you forgive others their trespasses, your heavenly Father will also forgive you; but if you do not forgive oth-

ers, neither will your Father forgive your trespasses.(Matt. 6:14-15).

If some doubt persists about how the ideal translates into the practical expression of life, Jesus further instructs his followers:

In everything do to others as you would have them do to you; for this is the law and the prophets (Matt. 7:12).

The theme of positive, caring relationships with other people is sustained throughout the New Testament. Romans 12:3, 10-21 spells it out well:
- do not think too highly of yourself
- love sincerely
- be devoted to one another
- honor one another
- share resources
- be hospitable
- bless those who treat you wrongly
- do not be proud or conceited
- do not repay evil for evil or seek revenge
- overcome evil with good

That is the type of Hi-Q Christians the church is expected to grow. Any congregation will rejoice when the number increases of members who live that type of relationship-oriented life.

Some pastors and theologians have taken a cue from personality theory and depth psychology and overstated the value

In all the growing churches studied, efforts were made to remind people that their responsibility was to be the church, not just to attend one.

—George Barna (1991, 72)

of loving oneself. Picking up on the phrase "Love your neighbor as yourself" these persons have often said that the key to loving people is grounded in the ability to love one's self. Certainly many persons, even millions of Christians, need help in learning to love themselves.

Jesus, however, does not seem to be convinced that self-love is a solution to life's problems. The first instruction is to center on God or reverence God; the second is to respect people (which includes ourselves). Jesus' teachings appear to presume that most of us are loving ourselves sufficiently but are not paying enough attention to God and other persons. Christianity does not begin with a love of oneself; that can lead to indulgence and license. The Christian faith begins with a love for God and follows with a discipline to respect and honor people. Probably the first and greatest commandment is the only sure foundation for self-esteem, from the Christian perspective.

BIBLICAL GUIDELINES FOR RELATIONSHIPS

We can teach respect for persons by following some biblical guidelines for relationships. Here are a few:

No "Top Ten"
1. *No "top ten" list of people exists.* It is our consistent sin to want to establish who are the best people and who are less than best. Paul warned us, as we have noted, not to think more highly of ourselves than we ought and to associate with people of all cultural levels.

In our culture people are absorbed with ratings like
- the top ten basketball teams
- the ten best-dressed women in America
- the *Fortune* 500 list
- the *New York Times* Bestseller list

We carry over into our Christian thinking and living the idea that some people are better than others. When we speak of Hi-Q Christians we do not mean a Christian elite who have

34

special privileges; we imply Christians who make a commitment to be servants.

When I was a child I heard the phrase, "That person needs to get off his high horse." Paul is saying that Christians do not lord it over each other. Unfortunately, Christians most certainly can do that, and here are some ways it is done, even in the life of the church:

• Some feel they are better because of family or traditions (it's who you know that counts).

• Some feel superior because of their education, or at least because of certificates that say they are educated.

• Some think of themselves as better than others because they possess exceptional amounts of money or property.

• Some think of themselves as better because they have "worked hard" to attain their position; others who do not have property or other security are judged as loafers.

• Some feel themselves spiritually superior (yes, it is true) because of a particular spiritual gift.

• Some Christians feel themselves to be "deeper" in spiritual matters, or more committed than the average Christian, and thus somehow better or special.

• Some may feel themselves better because they belong to a certain group of Christians or a particular denomination.

Any of these vain assumptions, however popular, are inconsistent with the spirit of Christ. The assumptions stray far from a humility grounded in a respect for people.

No One Perfect Perspective

2. *No one way to see anything and everything* If people viewed every situation the same, sports fans would never blast umpires and police would have an easy time solving crimes using identical eyewitness accounts. Nor does it help when we presume that persons would see things our way if they only used common sense. Logic is not the only way to see and analyze a situation. Some persons say the only safe way to view difficult situations is to ignore them and they will go away.

Perspectives can change. Stephen Covey tells about a Sunday morning when he was on a subway in New York City.

Passengers were reading newspapers or sitting peacefully and enjoying a casual day. Then a man got on with several children and chaos erupted. The children yelled at each other, bumped into other passengers, and grabbed at readers' newspapers. Covey could not understand why the father did not take control of his children.

Finally, in desperation, Covey spoke to the father and asked him to do something. The man appeared to awake from a stupor and offered his apologies. He explained that he and his children were coming from a hospital where their mother had died an hour before and he really did not know quite what to do. Immediately Covey began to talk with the man about his grief and about ways Covey might help. His perspective had changed (1989, 30-31).

Respect for persons means making a conscious effort to see situations as others see them.

Learn to Listen

3. *Wash your ears.* One of my elementary grade teachers used that phrase; so did my mother. I remember one day Jack was daydreaming in class when the teacher called on him for a comment. Jack was oblivious to her voice. Finally, when she got his attention, Jack said, "I'm sorry but I didn't hear you."

The teacher replied, "Then, Jack, we had better wash out your ears." The message came through loud and clear to me: I had better keep my ears washed out, also.

Listening to what people are saying and understanding their feelings are important parts of respecting them. Occasionally I have heard it said even of a Christian fellowship, "No one in that church ever hears what I say, or even cares."

Most of us have never learned how to listen. A husband and wife can talk for hours and not hear what the other is saying. Children give up in desperation after they have repeatedly talked to parents and realized they have not been heard.

We learn how to write. We learn how to talk. We learn how to carry on surface conversations. We learn how to make presentations. Public schools and colleges offer many courses on personal and creative expression. Rarely is a class offered on how to listen to another person.

It would be a marvelous day if, in the next decade it could be said of Christians, "They are people who care enough about you to listen to what you are saying." The church could take a cue from Dean Witter, the successful investment counselor who instructed his agents, "Listen not only to what our clients say, but to what they mean."

Respect for persons means we take time to really hear, really understand, and respond with empathy—feeling with them.

Everybody a Winner

4. *Let everybody win.* Counselors, family therapists, church consultants, and management specialists have all encouraged us over the past decade to get out of win/lose relationships and get into win/win patterns.

Competition in marriages, competition in families,competition in classrooms, and competition in churches tend to create a small number of winners and an abundance of losers; many times one person wins and *everyone* else loses.

The gospel suggests that everyone is a winner. Everyone is a candidate for God's grace. Everyone can pray. Everyone has promise of blessings. Everyone has a unique set of gifts that enables him or her to serve other persons in special and meaningful ways. Everyone has something to contribute. When anyone suffers then all grieve. When anyone rejoices, all are happy for that person.

The New Testament is rather insistent that the Christian community be structured so that everyone wins. In Christian relationships in the home and the church it is our task to let everyone win—to do our best to make sure everyone wins.

Allowing everyone to win takes more time; it is easier if one person gets what he or she wants and everyone else has to accommodate. For everyone to win, we must set aside selfish ways of boosting our own egos. It means we cannot judge our own success on the basis of someone else's loss—how we beat them.

> *We have a tendency to put people*
> *into categories—*
>
> > *that's "thingy"*
> > *that "thingizes" them-*
> > *it turns them into "its"*
> > *instead of "yous."*
>
> *You know how Southerners are.*
> *I do 'cause I'm not one.*
> *You know how Westerners are,*
> > *you know how the Mexican*
> > > *the Blacks*
> > > *the Orientals are.*
> *Put them into categories,*
> > *slip them into little slots*
> > *categorized*
> > *depersonalized*
> > *massed-up*
> > > *and that's not love.*
> *Love sees the person.*
> > > —Reuben Welch (1982, 96)

Stephen Covey's best selling book, *The Seven Habits of Highly Effective People,* insists that win/win is a pattern absolutely necessary for personal and public success. He speaks and writes for persons in business leadership and corporations. Surely the idea needs to be exercised in the church.

The message of win/win is at the heart of the gospel. Even the thief on the cross, a criminal, became a winner with Christ. Christians who will make a difference in the decade of the nineties and churches that will be catalysts for the kingdom of God in the twenty-first century will do well to capture the spirit and practice of win/win.

Real life is not even remotely like a ball game. It is possible for everyone to win in life:

• Everyone in a family can feel good about a decision if it is negotiated and responsible.

• A husband and wife can feel good about a decision if both participate in forming it.

• It is possible in the workplace for nearly every person to feel good about a situation and a decision, if each is included in the process.

• It is necessary in the church that we work together so that everyone has a sense of winning.

• Yes, even sports can be a winning experience for both persons or both teams, when we recover the attitude that intense participation in the game, in the fun, is the real purpose and benefit of a sport.

Providing a way for everyone to win is a way of respecting persons. It is a characteristic of Hi-Q Christians.

> *Win/Win is a frame of mind and heart that constantly seeks mutual benefit in all human interactions. Win/Win means that agreements or solutions are mutually beneficial, mutually satisfying. With a Win/Win solution, all parties feel good about the decision and feel committed to the action plan. Win/Win sees life as a cooperative, not a competitive arena. . . . Win/Win is based on the paradigm that there is plenty for everybody, that one person's success is not achieved at the expense or exclusion of the success of others. . . .It's not your way or my way; it's a better way, a higher way.*
> —Stephen R. Covey (1989, 207)

Pray for People

5. *Pray for persons by name.* When you or I pray for someone by name the relationship is elevated. A mysterious alchemy takes place. Prayer for a person gets us so involved that our respect for the person increases, even if our attitude had been one of animosity. Jesus had the audacity to tell us to pray for our enemies, and other persons who mistreat us.

When I stand before the Lord and ask the Lord to bless someone, I enter into that person's life at a dynamic level. When I take the time to know enough about persons that I can pray for them, for their hopes, their dreams, their needs and their goals, then I am respecting them as persons whom God loves. In the process I can come to love them, also.

We are not sure about the direct relationship of one person's prayers to the decision of another. There are times when the report of change is just too good to be coincidental. Recently Doris reminded me of the Sunday morning I had spoken in her home church. In my sermon I had stated that miracles are still in order, that some personal situations have no solution without the intervention of God and that each person should feel free to request of God that one special miracle he or she most desires.

That Sunday morning Doris was grieved and concerned that her son and his wife, the parents of her six-month-old grandchild, were getting a divorce. She was sure there was no hope, but she dared write her request for a reconciliation on a sheet of paper and place it on the altar. Six months later her former daughter-in-law was led to a personal relationship with Jesus Christ by a fellow worker. Some months later she and her husband, Doris's son, began to see each other again. Doris was all smiles as she concluded, "And this past Christmas they were married again. It's a miracle."

One may say, "Yes but they are her children and grandchild. She would naturally be concerned." The truth is that even spouses, parents, and children often show little respect for each other. Criticizing, ignoring, and verbally, if not physically, abusing relatives are too common. Prayer for persons is a dynamic life-changing option that demonstrates respect.

Not all prayers are answered so specifically and gloriously as was the prayer of Doris. Even so, prayer is one way Christians respect others; to genuinely pray for a friend, or an enemy, is a high expression of respect. And prayers are answered! Jesus told us so.

Patience with People

6. *Be patient with persons, even when you may be exasperated with them.* Each of us needs, occasionally, to be reminded of how patient God has been with us. Parents, teachers, employers, associates, spouses, and children have shown patience with each of us. (If we do not realize that, it is one of the reasons others are driven to exasperation.)

Patience with situations, with events, and in the accomplishment of tasks has its own rewards. Patience with people is a Christian virtue (Gal. 5:22). Patience is a definitive act of humility.

• We can be patient with persons in their differences. Children are not all alike and often are distinctly different in temperament and aspiration from their parents. In the church people are different. Too often the difference is immediately translated into prejudicial evaluations like "conservative," or "liberal," or differences may even be identified as "heresy," or "sin."

• We can be patient with persons in their rate of comprehension. Persons learn at different rates; some persons incorporate a new idea or an insight readily, others more slowly. Persons comprehend or apprehend the gospel on a variety of schedules.

• We can be patient with persons in their readiness to risk. Jesus himself taught that disciples should make sure they are willing to pay the cost before making a commitment (Luke 14:28). Not all persons take risks, including the risks of faith, easily.

• We can be patient with persons in their pilgrimages. People grow, travel, and learn at rates determined by their personality types, life experiences, and personal dreams, among other things. In the family and the church, especially, patience with each person on his or her spiritual journey is essential to the health of the individual and the group. We all need that patience.

Nearly ten years ago I became friends with Charles; I was his pastor. Contributing to our friendship was our common roots in West Virginia and my acquaintance with two of his brothers. Though our friendship grew, his attendance to worship services was sporadic. He was wounded by failed marriages and obviously had unresolved bitterness. He and a lovely Christian woman decided to marry and I counseled them and performed the ceremony. He claimed a saving relationship with Jesus Christ, but his attitude and the pattern of his life were not convincing.

Often we talked about his need to make a commitment to a serious walk with Christ. During a dinner out together, as a part of counseling and in casual conversations, I suggested that a vital relationship with Jesus Christ could be the foundation for beginning a beautiful new marriage and family relationship.

It became obvious a few months after they were married that harsh and critical words were too often a part of their conversation and she was doubtful their marriage could last. I continued to urge him to get his spiritual life straightened out, assuring him that many other things would improve as a result and I would help in every way of which I was capable. He made no positive moves. Quite frankly, I despaired he would ever make a change.

More than a year after I left that pastorate, his brother John, a pastor, sent me a card informing me my friend was being baptized. A year after that a note came from his wife with a statement of awe and amazement at the change that had come in his life. My wife and I both rejoiced; she had participated with me in their counseling sessions.

Bill McCartney, Coach of the Colorado University Buffaloes football team, keeps asking the readers of his autobiography for patience with him and with others. He confesses that after he became a born-again Catholic, a nagging drinking problem retarded his spiritual growth and influence. His language on the sidelines was also inconsistent with his claim to be a follower of Christ. McCartney, named Coach of the Year by the American Football Coaches Association following the 1989 season, says,

I confess I'm not the man I want to be, and I'm not the Christian I should be or hope to be—but I'm a struggling Christian who is growing and making progress; one who makes mistakes, yet wants his life to be the very best it can be before God Almighty (1990, 159).

Patience with persons may be trying or exasperating, but many people need extra and extended patience if they are to overcome hurtful forces in their lives.

Give 'Em Cookies

7. *Give 'em cookies, even when they treat you badly.* Respecting persons is rather easy if we only have to respect those who treat us well. Jesus challenged us even to be kind to someone who takes our coat or forces us to walk a mile carrying a burden.

Christian Wilson and his wife Betty were pastors of the only Christian congregation in Kabul, Afghanistan. They led the congregation in the construction of a lovely sanctuary. In time, the Islamic government forced the Wilsons to leave their congregation and the country. After the Wilsons had returned to America, the government ordered the people to abandon the building; it was going to be destroyed. Friends of the Wilsons were contacted throughout the world, urging them to pray for the church in Kabul. A miracle was needed to spare the one place of Christian worship in that city. The miracle never came. The Afghan military brought in bulldozers one day and began to destroy the church building. Something wonderful did happen, though. The congregation met the soldiers and the equipment that day at the church site and served them tea and cookies (MacDonald, 226-227).

Respect for persons, for the Christian, includes serving those who have misused us.

RESPECT BEGINS WITH ME

Respect of persons begins with me. If we want to make a difference in the family, the community, and the church, then we must begin with a humility that respects all persons. We cannot expect someone else to do this task for us.

Lynn and Marie Stuart were my hosts for three weeks during one of my assignments in Portland, Oregon. Their home is equipped with an exercise room complete with a motorized treadmill, stationary bicycle, and a rowing machine. It is my intent to exercise thirty minutes at least three times a week. The exercise room was right next to my bedroom, so each morning I could get up, turn on the treadmill, go upstairs and eat breakfast, read the paper, and then come back downstairs and turn off the treadmill. It is a delightful way to take care of my exercises. I have even considered buying one for my home. It would help my wife greatly. You see, I have been suggesting that she demonstrate her love for me by getting up on some mornings and walking two miles for me, for she knows my physician has said I need that exercise.

The idea of doing exercises that way is, of course, ridiculous. It is just as ridiculous for me (or you) to keep waiting for others to accept those spiritual disciplines that no one else can do for us. Respect for persons includes respect for ourselves, and it is a humble and difficult discipline.

FOR MEDITATION OR DISCUSSION

1. What are your pet peeves about people? What consistently aggravates you about others?

Do you tend to speak degradingly and harshly about
other persons in your conversations with family and
friends? If you do, Why?

2. What factors in your life make you feel positive about
yourself?

- wealth
- hard work
- physical abilities
- wisdom
- your practice of the faith
- Other:

- talents
- winsome personality
- reasoning power
- education
- church membership

Which of these factors, if any, have the reverse effect of
making you feel negative about other persons (at least
less respectful)?

3. Do you always need to win? Or, do you frequently man-
age to lose?   What changes would you need to make in your

relationship patterns to enable you to be a winner and help others be winners, also?

4. Identify four ways you can improve your listening skills.
-
-
-
-

5. In what areas of your life do you need the joy and exercise of more patience? Marriage, family, work place, school, national leaders, the pastor(s), friends, the one you are dating or your fiancé / fiancée?

6. List five persons to whom you will express respect with words of appreciation or a compliment or to whom you will give some time in conversation or service.

Names   How will you make your expression?

4

Generous

Hi-Q Christians are generous. The New Testament and history suggest that a committed follower of Jesus Christ is generous in sharing material and spiritual blessings. A consistent characteristic in the life of high quality Christians is generosity.

A GENEROUS ATTITUDE

Generosity is an attitude. The Corinthians learn that the model for generosity is Jesus Christ. He was rich, yet became like us, poor. His purpose was that we too might be rich. Paul wrote to the Philippians, "Your attitude should be the same as that of Christ Jesus ... who made himself nothing" (Phil. 2:5, 7, NIV).

Generosity is an attitude we have toward people. We put ourselves in their position and understand them and try to help them. Recently I returned from a trip to learn that Sam Trick, an elderly friend of mine, had died. His death reminded me of an experience I had when I was in seminary. Laura was teaching school, we had two little girls, and I was supplementing our income with odd jobs—doing pulpit supply work on weekends and working on a college remodeling crew in the summer. I was attempting to finish my studies in twenty months.

I recalled that once Sam had telephoned in the middle of the week and asked if I would help him install gutters at a home on the west side of town. I jumped at the chance to earn three or maybe even four or five dollars. He picked me up on Saturday morning. I knew nothing about metal work or installing gutters but I helped him for about three hours. When we completed the job he handed me twenty-five dollars. I protested that what I had done was not worth that much. Sam said, "I want to help." I have never forgotten the generosity of Sam Trick or dozens of others who have gone out of their way to help me. They have a generous attitude.

Some months ago I visited The Church at the Crossing in Indianapolis. The church has an attractive and functional educational building and a lovely sanctuary, at that time under construction. More than seven hundred persons are present for worship each Sunday and improved facilities would permit additional growth. One would think the reason that local church is present and serving in the community is because a few people with a lot of money gave to establish the church. But that is not correct.

One would think that the reason the church has missions efforts in countries throughout the world is because some wealthy persons have established an endowment to pay missionary salaries. The truth is, most missionaries now have to raise their own salaries before leaving for the field. Local churches and all the ministries and missions efforts in which they are involved in cities, in states, and around the world are a result of Christians who have a generous attitude. These persons have identified with the needy people of the world and want to help. Some generous persons are poor, some live on average incomes, and a few might be called wealthy. One reason churches, ministries, and missions are started, sustained, and result in significant advances for the kingdom of God is generosity. Were it not for people with a generous attitude the church would have to stop most of its ministries.

A television commercial comes to mind of a fluffy toy rabbit. The commercial may begin with a sea diving excursion or an animal that is the symbol of an investment firm. Suddenly

During a severe ordeal of affliction, their abundant joy and their extreme poverty have overflowed in a wealth of generosity on their part. For, as I can testify, they voluntarily gave according to their means, and even beyond their means, begging us earnestly for the privilege of sharing in this ministry to the saints— and this, not merely as we expected; they gave themselves first to the Lord and, by the will of God, to us, so that we might urge Titus that, as he had already made a beginning, so he should also complete this generous undertaking among you. Now as you excel in everything—in faith, in speech, in knowledge, in utmost eagerness, and in our love for you—so we want you to excel also in this generous undertaking.
—2 Corinthians 8:2-7

the rabbit appears, beating his drum and powered by Energizer batteries. The announcer says, "Still going."

Generous persons in every church keep the gospel alive in their community. Go with me to Sikeston, Missouri. I have not pastored there for years but I know you will find Kenneth and Bonnie still giving generously, still going. Or go to Columbus, Ohio, and you will find Larry and Patty still giving generously, still going. Go on out to Casper, Wyoming. Bill and Helen are still giving generously, and still going. Generosity is an attitude, an attitude like that of Jesus Christ and those people in the Macedonian church who "gave themselves first to the Lord and then to us in keeping with God's will."

EXCELLENCE

Generosity is excellence. The Christians in the city of Corinth were achievers; when they did things they did them well. They undoubtedly had a variety of spiritual gifts. If they had had a church softball team, it would have won the city championship. They excelled in everything having to do with church. They were great in faith. They could give a testimony, sermon, or a lesson on cue. They had knowledge of the Word. They were earnest and loving. They were about as perfect as a church could get in some ways. Paul tells them that if they are really going to be excellent they will also excel in giving.

We have to face two questions when we consider exceptional generosity, excellent giving. First, we do not give in order to get a financial return. I know of nothing in the New Testament that suggests that if we give a thousand dollars to the church we can soon count on driving a baby-blue Cadillac or Chevrolet sports van. That is a manipulative promise and has nothing to do with the Christian stewardship Paul encourages. We do not give in order to receive a financial return on investment. Even so, I believe that often generosity results in a use of funds that permits unusual material blessings. Jim, a friend of mine, shared at a men's prayer breakfast that his family at one time was not able to live on his salary, one he described as good. Jim and his wife accepted Christ, he explained, and began to give a significant offering each Sunday as a part of their worship. Jim said, "Since then, it is amazing that we have learned how to use the money we have and now are able to afford some purchases that were not possible for us before." He concluded, "Don't ask me to tell you how that happens, but that is the way it has been for us."

The other question has to do with tithing. John came to me several years ago and said, "Pastor, I am not going to make a commitment to our building fund. I tithe and if everyone in our church tithed, we would not have to have a building fund campaign." What he said is exactly true. But John at that time misunderstood Christian stewardship.

Generous persons are not satisfied with tithing. Generosity

51

is an attitude, a practice, a way of life that moves beyond tithing. Tithing is a beginning, however, and tithing can be a shocking experience to new Christians in at least five ways:

1. It is a shock when a Christian learns that tithing means giving ten percent of one's income.

2. It is a shock when a Christian learns that the Bible teaches tithing (Malachi 3:8-10, Matthew 23:23).

3. It is a shock to learn the pastor tithes.

4. It is a shock to learn all Christians are expected to tithe.

5. It is a shock to learn some Christians do tithe but most Christians do not.

In our early years of ministry, my husband and I were involved in planting a church. Since most of the persons financially supporting the work would place their tithes and offerings in the offering plate on Sunday morning, there were a few Sunday evenings when not a cent would appear. On one such occasion the plate was passed down several rows and then came to a child. As she peered into the empty offering plate, her eyes grew large and looking up to her aunt sitting next to her said loudly, "Someone's gotta pay!"

—JoRene Nevitt (1991, 2)

Though tithing may be a surprising teaching of Scripture, the high quality Christian who is needed in this decade and the coming century will not stop with a tithe. The high quality Christian who makes a difference will be obviously and repeatedly generous in relationships with people and in the use of material resources. Excellence in Christian living includes excellence in Christian giving.

John Templeton, regarded as one of the world's wisest investors and founder of the Templeton mutual fund group, manages six billion dollars for more than 500,000 investors. His daughter Dr. Anne Zimmerman told me that Templeton encourages people to tithe and prays each day for divine direction in all of his decisions. He says, "Giving leads to greater giving and becomes a way of life," and, "Thanksgiving inspires giving, not only in the person who is thankful but in the one who hears the thanksgiving. . . . Thanksgiving opens the door to spiritual progress." Templeton believes that "Those who are full of thanksgiving are givers, and the successful are grateful givers." (2)

COMPLETENESS

Generosity is completeness. Paul encourages the people in Corinth to "finish the work." It is a challenge to do what we promised the Lord when he saved us, or healed us, or got us out of a jam, or relieved our mind, or rescued us in any way.

We will never be the person God has created us to be until we learn and practice generosity. When we practice generosity we may be surprised at the miracles God performs.

On a recent trip to Phoenix, I visited the Mountain Park Community Church. The pastor, my son-in-law Robin Wood, asked me to tell a group of about fifty persons gathered for a Sunday evening session about what it means to make a faith promise. Some churches use this method to raise mission funds. During my brief presentation I encouraged the people to indicate the next Sunday the amount of money they would pass on for missions, if the Lord provided it. I suggested that often a husband and wife would arrive at the same figure independently.

A couple, an engineer and his wife, were present, in part because I, Carma's dad, was going to be there and they like Carma, Robin and their three children. They were not Christians and had been hesitant in their response to efforts to get them interested in the church.

The husband liked the dare involved in "the Lord providing the money." For the fun of it, he asked his wife what she thought they should promise. She said five hundred dollars and thought he would suggest a much lower figure, but he had the same amount in mind. They ruled out everything they could think of as a way to pay this promise such as a tax return, a pay raise, and a gift from their parents. They really wanted this to be money provided in an unexpected way.

The next day he went to the office. He was at his desk when the accountant came around and told him that he had exceeded the limit set for his retirement fund that year and, thus, he would receive a refund in the next four pay checks. When Mike added the amounts of the four checks he realized the total would be five hundred dollars.

This engineer, perhaps a bit callous toward religious things, started crying. He kept crying, and finally talked with his boss and went home. He called my daughter, told her that he had accepted Christ, and told her the story. He apologized to his wife and children for some wrong attitudes and actions toward them and told Robin the next day they would start tithing the next Sunday. Sometime later the church had a building fund campaign and this new convert made a significant additional financial commitment.

When we agree to be generous, we are opening ourselves to graces and blessings that we never thought could happen. When we are generous, the Lord can use us in fantastic, miracle producing ways.

One of my favorite stories is about a young school teacher who was present when a superintendent of the Methodist Church was the visiting preacher at a little congregation on the Pearl River in Mississippi more than 150 years ago. The preacher told the people about the need for missions, missionaries, and missions support. As was the custom, the congregation received an offering at the end of the service. In the plate was a note wrapped around some money. The note read, "I give $5 and myself. Mary I. McClellan." The offering was a generous one for that day and greatly appreciated. The Methodist ministers did not know what to do with Mary

McClellan. The Missionary Board did not want to consider a sixteen-year-old single woman for missions service. They were wringing their hands for she insisted the Lord called her.

A young man in Alabama named James Lambuth was to solve their problem. When James was born his dad was preaching for a camp meeting. The dad heard the news of the birth of his baby boy and dedicated him to missionary service and vowed a bale of cotton with which to send him.

Young James Lambuth and Mary were married and went to China. They both had a marvelous ministry, though often in very difficult situations. Mary kept sending letters back to America begging for money from the Missions Board, but the Civil War had started and money was scarce. A young bride heard of Mary's need, took off her wedding jewelry, sold it, and sent the proceeds to Mary. Her action help build a girls' school in China and led to the establishment of the Methodist women's missionary society.

Mary and James had a son after they arrived in Shanghai, during the Boxer Rebellion. The young boy observed his mother and father as he grew and was deeply impressed. Walter Lambuth gave himself to the missionary cause and became the missionary bishop in China and ministered on several continents (Applegarth 1957, 80-83).

That is what can happen when we practice generosity. God can use all that we give to minister to needy people. High quality Christians like the Lambuths are needed in this decade, as we prepare for the next century.

FOR MEDITATION OR DISCUSSION

1. Which of the following prayers would be your prayer?
   • Lord, I've been generous; please help me continue.
   • Lord, I want to be generous. Help me overcome what-ever makes me afraid and hesitant to be generous.
   • Lord, I am stingy. Save me from stinginess and help me take the risks of generosity.
   • Lord, help me to see people's needs—human and spiritual—and help me to become aware of ways I can help meet them.
   • Lord, give me courage to do what you have been calling me to do with my life, with my money, with my whole personality.
   • Lord, this is my prayer: (write in your own words)

2. Two persons in the first-century church got into serious trouble over their financial gift. They were Ananias and Sapphira and you will find their story in the Book of Acts 5.
   What misunderstandings do you think this couple had?

Why do you think they responded as they did to Peter?

Do members of the church today behave like this couple?

How does God respond today to Christians who are not faithful in their stewardship?

3. Generous persons are a pleasure to know. Some of your friends are generous.

Name a friend who is generous in contributions to the
   church and other agencies that serve people:

Name a friend who is generous with compliments:

Name a friend who is generous in thinking and speaking
   the best about other persons:

Name a friend who is generous in offering a helping
   hand:

4. Have you ever had an unanticipated blessing in your life
as a result of a generous gift or act on your part? How did it
come about?

5. What steps can a new Christian take toward becoming
generous?
   • If the person has been raised in a family that sought to
     retain material blessings for themselves?

   • If the new Christian has never thought to give kind and
     encouraging comments to other persons?

   • If the new Christian wants to be vitally involved in the
     total mission and ministry of the local church?

5

Accountable

The Accounting Department is located on the floor below my office in the Board of Church Extension and Home Missions building in Anderson, Indiana. Checks, money orders, sometimes stocks and bonds, and some cash are sent to that office every day. Hundreds of people invest their savings with the understanding that as much as possible will be loaned to churches to build sanctuaries, educational facilities, or family life centers.

More than forty persons work in our offices, including persons who direct building fund campaigns, give guidance to church planting and church growth, and administer home missions. Still others are home missionary personnel or directors of metropolitan ministries. Money comes in for all of these ministries and is honestly and accurately recorded, no guesses.

Money is distributed to congregations so that they can build. Money is sent to investors to pay the interest they were promised when they loaned some of their life savings; not one of these persons wants an approximate amount in a check. The job of the accounting office is to hold everyone specifically responsible in matters of finance.

Laura, my wife, has a similar responsibility in our home. At least once a month she looks at the checkbook and makes sure the amount we have deposited with the bank reasonably matches the amount we have spent or are going to spend.

> *I therefore, the prisoner in the Lord, beg you to lead a life worthy of the calling to which you have been called, with all humility and gentleness, with patience, bearing with one another in love, making every effort to maintain the unity of the Spirit in the bond of peace.*
> —Ephesians 4:1-3

Occasionally she and I talk about our budget to make sure each of us is responsible in the expenditure of available finances. We have found accountability to be a much more comfortable experience than the chaos that erupts when we have forgotten to be accountable.

Good coaches hold team members accountable. Parents teach and expect accountability. Employers build accountability into job and position descriptions.

Christians, also, are accountable. That may seem to be an obvious statement, unnecessarily redundant. Too many of us Christians, however, act independently, not wanting to be held responsible for the way we live. Too many of us seem to live as we please and act as if it were an invasion of privacy to suggest that Christians are accountable. We may even suggest we are accountable only to God and, of course, imply that God has given total approval to the way we are living.

THE BIBLE

The Bible is one guide for accountability. Christians are accountable to the spirit and words of Jesus, but the writings of Paul and the other apostles, also, are written for our guidance. Paul says,

All scripture is inspired by God and is useful for teaching, for reproof, for correction, and for training in righteousness, so that every one who belongs to God may be proficient, equipped for every good work (2 Timothy 3:16).

CONSCIENCE

The conscience is another guide for accountability. One Old Testament prophet spoke of the day that the law of God would be written on our hearts (Jereriah 31:31-34). We know from observation and personal experience that a conscience can be trained, made callous, or repeatedly ignored and thus become inoperative. Even with persons who retain an open, or tender, conscience, one has to beware that it can be used as an excuse ("my conscience is clear") rather than as a reliable guide. Paul knew the riskiness of relying solely on the conscience. He said that even when his conscience was clear, that did not mean he was innocent (1 Corinthians 4:4).

When I was a toddler I saw a large toy truck left unattended in front of Mr. Bailey's Grocery. No one was playing with it so I told myself I had found it and thus it was mine. I had been taught not to steal but my conscience, though bothersome and inconvenient even at an early age, could be adjusted to fit the occasion. Fortunately, I was quickly instructed by my mother in no uncertain terms to return the truck immediately.

The Bible and our conscience are superb sources for accountability, but we can perform amazing mental gymnastics with both to validate our behavior. You may know, as I do, persons who have committed adultery and used scripture and conscience to excuse their actions. Others have misused funds, supposedly under God's direction, and some have even brought bodily harm to others, all in good conscience. Scriptures intended for instruction in righteousness are often perverted and used as a justification for sin, such as, "since all have sinned and fall short of the glory of God" (Romans 3:23) and Jesus' words to the group who were ready to stone the woman taken in adultery, "Let anyone among you who is without sin be the first to throw a stone at her" (John 8:7). Both of these scriptures encourage a mature understanding of

> **You were taught to put away your former way of life, your old self, corrupt and deluded by its lusts, and to be renewed in the spirit of your minds, and to clothe yourselves with the new self, created according to the likeness of God in true righteousness and holiness.**
>
> —Ephesians 4:22-24

the grace and love of God, not an escape hatch for those who want an excuse for their sins.

Most of us are tempted to use the Bible and conscience conveniently; it is difficult to understand how either could be used to justify adultery, dishonesty, or injury to another. All of us need some additional guides for living the Christian life.

MEMBERSHIP, SMALL GROUPS, AND PASTOR

The Lord has provided at least three other guides for accountability, in addition to the Bible and our conscience:

1. Membership in the body of Christ, the church, is a structure for accountability. In the story of the first-century church we read of three thousand people being saved on one occasion. The historian of the early church, Luke, explains that these persons
- met in the temple daily
- gave close attention to the apostle's teachings
- participated in the fellowship
- broke bread together
- prayed together
- shared material possessions
- praised God
- observed wonders and signs (Acts 2:37-47)

> *So then, putting away falsehood, let all of us speak the truth to our neighbors, for we are members of one another. Be angry but do not sin; do not let the sun go down on your anger.... Thieves must give up stealing; ... Let no evil talk come out of your mouths, but only what is useful for building up. ... Put away from you all bitterness and wrath and anger and wrangling and slander, together with all malice, and be kind to one another, tenderhearted, forgiving one another, as God in Christ has forgiven you.*
>
> —Portions of Ephesians 4:25-32

The Lone Ranger was a fictitious masked cowboy who in past decades was the hero of movies, radio, and comic books. Single-handedly, or at times with the help of his faithful partner Tonto, he was able to bring law and order to frontier communities. He was a mystery man who always appeared on the scene in times of trouble, handled the job of ridding the area of crooks by himself, and then disappeared, riding his horse into the sunset with a mighty "Hi-o, Silver, away!"

Christians who want to operate independently of any fellowship, any local church, and do their own thing, have sometimes been called Lone Ranger Christians.

The scriptures indicate quite clearly that a Lone Ranger approach to Christian living is not acceptable. The Christian life is not something one can live by himself or herself.

Joining God's church is not even something we decide to do. As Luke records the habits of the first century church he adds, "Day by day the Lord added to their number those who were being saved" (Acts 2:47). We can make a choice about the local group of Christians with whom we choose to be accountable. As a Christian, we do not have the option of deciding whether or not we will be accountable to a group. God has a place for each of us in the church and we are mutually accountable with other Christians.

God has placed you and me in the church because he knows that we need an organic, alive, accountable relationship with other persons who have accepted the same salvation and made similar commitments to be followers of Christ.

2. Participation in a small group of Christians is another relationship in which a Christian is accountable. Some congregations identify their membership requirements very precisely. Even so, when you or I get into a group of more than fifteen or so people it is quite easy for us to fool ourselves and each other. Each of us can pretend to be spending time in prayer, scripture study, and moral living. Each of us can harbor bitter and resentful attitudes, let them fester, and yet smile as if nothing is bothering us, communicating that everything in our inner life is totally acceptable. It has been known to happen. However, neither you nor I can fool a mutually committed small group of persons very long.

Three types of small groups help to hold Christians accountable. They are

• A small fellowship group of eight to fifteen Christians that meets regularly to pray with one another and grow together in the Lord is a rewarding accountability group. A warning: no small group is an adequate substitute for participation in the life of a congregation; when a small group is a substitute for the congregation it is inevitably destructive, harmful both to the persons in the group and to the church as a whole.

• A spiritual guide, adviser, or counselor can help us be accountable for the quality of our Christian life. A small group of two is too small unless one is selected by the other as a spiritual guide. Such a mentor should be of unquestioned maturity in the broader Christian fellowship and should willingly accept the role to guide a less experienced, younger brother or sister for a time. It is usually best that persons in this relationship be of the same sex so as to avoid any temptations to compromise

> *No man should be alone when he opposes Satan. The church and the ministry of the Word were instituted for this purpose, that hands may be joined together and one may help another. If the prayer of one doesn't help the prayer of another will.*
>
> —Martin Luther (28)

a spiritual relationship with inappropriate sexual overtones. A change in the relationship can take place even between persons with the best of intentions. A spiritual guide can insist on honesty in faith practices and offer counsel during difficult personal problems.

• *The family* can be one of the most helpful small groups if the members hold each other accountable, and if each member, including the father and mother, agrees to be accountable. One spouse or parent may attempt to hold all others to his or her personal standards; such is not a good family accountability structure. A better structure is each member of a family agreeing to listen intently when attitudes and actions are evaluated in light of the scripture and the teachings of the church. It is probably safe to say that parents who listen to the observations of their children will improve their personal discipleship and have the additional reward of having their children return for guidance after they are adults.

3. *The role of one special person is key in the accountability structure for Christians: the pastor.* As indicated before, one of the purposes of the church is to hold each of us accountable. It holds us accountable for beliefs and practices.

The local church keeps us responsible in many ways:
- the worship service on Sunday calls us to praise God, offer confession, and petitions
- the teachings of the church, whether written creeds or traditional interpretations of scriptures, remind us of

the basic tenets of our faith
- participation in the fellowship brings to mind our peculiar and special role in the kingdom of God
- the organization informs us of our ministry and financial responsibility in the group

The pastor is a key in this whole accountability structure God has created. The scriptures give explicit instructions about the pastor's responsibility.

The pastor is a person who
- has sensed a call of God to speak the gospel and guide the spiritual pilgrimages of believers;
- has been observed by both lay persons and experienced clergy to have demonstrated gifts for pastoral ministry;
- has studied the scriptures, doctrine, culture, psychology and dozens of other subjects for years and learned to relate these disciplines to the needs of the whole person;
- has gone through years of practical training under the scrutiny of experienced pastors;
- has been ordained, recognized by the church in a biblical pattern, as having been called by God and ready for the pastoral role.

Paul was inspired to write at least three books of the New Testament to help pastors know how to pastor, 1 and 2 Timothy and Titus. Pastors are ordained by God and certified by the church to hold each of us accountable for our quality of Christian living.

Pastors are responsible to hold us accountable
- through their sermons
- in teaching sessions
- by personal training sessions and by developing apprentice relationships
- through counseling: guiding thoughts, encouraging serious decisions
- in personal conversations
- through administrative structures
- by example, and if these are not adequate,
- through gentle, Christlike, personal confrontation.

> *But we appeal to you brothers and sisters, to respect those who labor among you, and have charge of you in the Lord and admonish you; esteem them very highly in love because of their work.*
>
> —1 Thessalonians 5:12-13

Of course the pastor is not solely responsible for accountability in the local church, but more than any other person the pastor is responsible to see that accountability takes place or is not neglected. It is not a role that wise pastors will readily demand; it is a pastoral and leadership function that wise congregations encourage their pastors to accept.

I NEED TO BE ACCOUNTABLE

What then are the areas of my faith for which I need to be held accountable? These paragraphs will be made personal so that I am not tempted to preach but rather confess my need as one among many who have a similar need for accountability.

My home congregation is Park Place Church but my speaking and teaching responsibilities require me to travel many weekends, often worshiping with other congregations. I am a member of Park Place Church and attend its worship services with my wife when I am home.

My pastor's name is Don. He has been a friend and colleague many more years than he has been my pastor. Nonetheless, he is my pastor and serves me well, inquiring about my health and my family often.

In what ways is it appropriate for the fellowship of believers at Park Place Church to hold me accountable? How should Don hold me accountable for both my private and public faith?

I have a good deal of freedom, and first of all I need to acknowledge my freedom in Christ and accept it. Paul gave extensive instructions to the Corinthian church and many of the instructions were quite specific. Paul knew that the law—that is, a list of things that they had to do and a list of things they could not do—would simply destroy Christians. So the element of generous freedom was repeatedly interjected into what he said. It is summarized well here:

"All things are lawful," but not all things are beneficial. "All things are lawful," but not all things build up. Do not seek your own advantage, but that of the other. . . . So, whether you eat or drink, or whatever you do, do everything for the glory of God (1 Corinthians 10:23-24, 31).

Paul encourages a thoughtful concern for other persons and a conscious commitment to God, but at the same time I am assured the body of Christ, the church, will not constantly try to force me into a restrictive mold.

I can decide whether I am going to accept this whole idea

Be careful then how you live, not as unwise people but as wise, making the most of the time, because the days are evil. So do not be foolish, but understand what the will of the Lord is. Do not get drunk with wine, for that is debauchery; but be filled with the Spirit, as you sing psalms and hymns and spiritual songs among yourselves, singing and making melody to the Lord in your hearts, giving thanks to God the Father at all times and for everything in the name of our Lord Jesus Christ.

Be subject to one another out of reverence for Christ.

—Ephesians 5:15-21

of freedom and accountability. Catch here the marvelous opportunity offered me in this scripture. "Be subject to one another out of reverence for Christ" (Ephesians 5:21, NRSV).

I do not have to submit to the church, to my family, to a group, or to my pastor. Of course, when I choose not to submit then I will reap the consequence of my actions. Submission is something that I choose to do. I know that if my life is to bring praise to Christ and I am going to be what God created me to be, then I must take advantage of these accountability relationships God has created to help me.

Park Place Church, my family, my small group, and especially Don, my pastor, have the right, even the responsibility, to hold me accountable in four specific ways:

1. My church and my pastor have the responsibility to hold me accountable for *worship*. They cannot track my worship experiences on a day-to-day basis nor can they know my attitude unless I tell them. They can, however, observe whether I am in worship services with the body of Christ. They can express concern about absences. I know my pastor is called by

> *Although Thomas did not believe in the resurrection of the Lord, he kept faithful to the community of the apostles. In that community the Lord appeared to him and strengthened his faith . . . . the name of Thomas means "twin," as the Gospel says, ... all of us are "two people," a doubting one and a believing one. We need the support and love of our brothers and sisters to prevent our doubting person from becoming dominant and destroying our capacity for belief.*
>
> —Henri J. M. Nouwen (1976, 56-57)

> ***Persons with a neurotic or psychotic religious experience avoid accountability by seeking out leaders who will give them detailed orders for life, thus relieving them personally of the responsibility for choices and sins. The mentally and socially sick Christian simply cops out on accountability, letting other persons make religious and moral choices for them. Fellow Christians may hold us accountable but are not accountable in our stead.***
>
> —Oral Withrow

God to do just that, to be my spiritual shepherd. My church and pastor can hold me accountable for public worship and my family and a small group may inquire more personally about my faithfulness to private times of worship.

2. My church and my pastor have the responsibility to hold me accountable for my *life-style.* The way I use my time, personality, and finances is not my business alone, since I am a Christian. My moral life and my business practices are a valid concern of my church and pastor. I have great freedom but the pastor can preach the truth and I need to be aware of the truth he or she preaches about my stewardship of life. My family and my group or spiritual adviser can help me avoid both moral and spiritual pitfalls if I mutually submit with them in a covenant relationship.

3. My church and my pastor have the responsibility to hold me accountable for my *ministry.* Four scriptures provide partial lists of ministry gifts and clearly teach that each Christian in the body of Christ has at least one gift—a way or several ways of ministering to and through the church:

Romans 12　　　　　　Ephesians 4
1 Corinthians 12　　　 1 Peter 4

I need my Christian friends to
- enable me to discover my spiritual gifts
- encourage me to accept my spiritual gifts
- challenge me to use my gifts in ministry.

4. My church and my pastor have a responsibility to hold me accountable for *relationships*. I may be tempted to pout. I will be prone to evaluate persons on the basis of my prejudices. I probably will want persons to accept me as I am and be reluctant to accept them for who they are. Whatever my weaknesses, I need my family, my pastor, my friends, my small

> *Church historian Martin Marty [speaks of] "pick-and choose Christianity." Kenneth Woodward reports that in one study that had 1,017 respondents, two-thirds "saw no harm in rejecting some of their church's doctrines." One woman said, "You sort out what you want and pick it apart as you see fit."*
> —Stephen Arterburn and Jack Felton (1941, 22)

group to help me be responsible for the way I relate to people and kindly, yet firmly, to challenge me when I am relating in an immature way that stops conversation, handshakes, smiles, and general communication. I know that I need this accountability more than many others.

I choose to be accountable because I want to be in my place and ready to act when I am needed.

Though not a gifted athlete, I have enjoyed sports all my life. Most are now spectator sports for me and I was thrilled recently when my hosts told me they had a seat for me to watch the Portland Trailblazers play the Utah Jazz, both championship teams with big name stars in the National Basketball Association. Portland won in the last second, 110-107. It was amazing to watch Clyde Drexler dribble the ball right into the midst of two or three opponents, realize there was no way through, and flip the ball backwards without looking. Each time I knew when Drexler passed the ball it had gone to the opponent but invariably a teammate moved to the right spot, took the ball, and continued the play. At the last split second and at the very spot needed, the player was there.

At other times John Stockton, of the Jazz, would be leading a fast break and two or three opponents would be blocking the way to the goal. Stockton would pass the ball between the opponents to what appeared to be an empty space but at just the precise moment the ball arrived so did teammate Karl Malone, "The Mailman," and the result was two points. They call Malone "The Mailman" because he always delivers.

These professional athletes trained for hours to be in the right spot when needed. The coach had time after time taught these players how to be accountable for what happens on the basketball floor and they were willing students.

When the tough times come in my life I want to be ready to handle them. When my family needs me I want to be in a position to assist them. When my church is depending on me I want to be in the right place. When my God needs my witness, my faithfulness, I want to be there. For these reasons, I often pray:

Please hold me accountable, church. Pastor, please hold me accountable. Family, please hold me accountable. Dear friend, hold me accountable. I will fail miserably if I do not have your help. God has given you to me to help me, and me to you. I want to live for my Lord in responsible and effective ways.

FOR MEDITATION OR DISCUSSION

1. Do you have a special Christian friend to whom you have given permission to hold you accountable?

If so, in what matters are you accountable to this person?

How often do you meet to talk about your spiritual life?

2. What events or activities of your local church best help you keep alert to your spiritual needs and disciplines?
- the sermon
- a small group
- study of beliefs
- other:
- a Sunday school class
- studies in a book of order
- reminders of standards

3. Are members of your family presently accountable to each other for spiritual disciplines?

Would your family or some members of your family be willing to become accountable to each other?

4. In what area of your Christian life do you need most help?

- worship
- personal ministry
- personal prayer time
- other:

- life-style
- relationships
- stewardship

5. In what matters would you expect your pastor to hold you personally accountable for your Christian life and disciplines:

- Through the sermon:

- Through teaching:

- Through conversation:

- Through counseling:

- Through confrontation:

6

Mature

One of the funniest sights I have ever seen on a stage was in a community benefit variety show when two grown men appeared dressed in diapers, bibs, and hair ribbons, holding oversized lollipops and baby bottles while making baby sounds. Their hairy legs and bulk made the scene hilariously funny, but it was also grotesque.

The scriptures suggest it is inappropriate for Christians to remain spiritual infants. Maturity is expected, almost demanded, by the Apostle Paul. He writes to some for whom he has special concern and responsibility:

> And so, brothers and sisters, I could not speak to you as spiritual people, but rather as people of the flesh, as infants in Christ. I fed you with milk, not solid food, for you were not ready for solid food. Even now you are still not ready, for you are still of the flesh. For as long as there is jealousy and quarreling among you, are you not of the flesh, and behaving according to human inclinations? (1 Cor. 3:1-3).

The author of Hebrews states the same idea with a more philosophical perspective:

> Therefore let us go on toward perfection, leaving behind

74

the basic teaching about Christ, and not laying again the foundation: repentance from dead works and faith toward God, instruction about baptisms, laying on of hands, resurrection of the dead, and eternal judgment. And we will do this, if God permits (Heb. 6:1-3).

Paul's letter boldly calls the Corinthian Christians to grow up and not remain babies in spiritual and church matters. The passage from Hebrews is a bit more difficult to understand because all the elemental statements that are mentioned are orthodox beliefs and concerns. Must we get beyond them, also? The answer is, Yes! The author is not suggesting these concerns are unimportant but that maturing Christians have to get beyond discussing the same things over and over again.

A friend of mine took me to his Sunday school class. During the discussion a gentleman to our right began to speak. My friend leaned over and said, "Watch it; somehow he is going to get the correct method of baptism into this discussion." The speaker did just as my friend said. Later the friend explained that this man could not participate in any group without attempting to persuade everyone of his particular view of baptism.

Some persons get stuck forever on a particular group of teachings about salvation, others cannot accept anyone else's view on how the world will end, and still others love to talk about the intricacies of the various doctrines of righteousness.

All of these subjects are important. Maturity, however, as we shall see, suggests that a Christ-like spirit and a compassionate heart are far more important than doctrinal exactness and conformity. Though of an anabaptist and Wesleyan tradition, I have been awed at the spiritual quality exhibited by some of my Calvinist friends. To put it more simply, as a young Christian I was very suspicious of anyone's spirituality who did not attend my church. In my own pilgrimage, however, I have come to appreciate the insights and witness of persons from groups as dissimilar from mine as the Catholic Church. The writings of Henri J. M. Nouwen, a Catholic, have been a tremendous resource for my spiritual life. I had to get beyond my sincere and convinced belief that no one who attended a Catholic church could tell me how to live for Jesus. I still have foundational beliefs and practices of faith that are different from persons of other churches, but I had to work past a prejudice that blinded me to the real essence of my religion—having faith in Christ and living as he taught.

WHAT DOES IT MEAN TO BE A BABE IN CHRIST?

Nothing is wrong with being a baby. Babies are cute, cuddly, and fantastic evidence of God's marvelous creative power. The same is true of babes in Christ. New converts are delightful to be around; they are so appreciative of the concern shown for them by friends in the church, and they are evidence of the saving power of Jesus Christ. The church enjoys having a lot of babes in Christ around, persons who have recently made a commitment to Christ and are beginning to grow in the Lord.

Problems develop in homes when a first grader wants to continue to stay home and not go to school, a teen-ager repeatedly pouts at the prospect of a chore, a husband wants to be waited on hand and foot, or a wife manipulates family members to get her way. One may expect such acts by a baby, much less from adolescents, and rarely from adults.

Problems develop for individual Christians and churches when persons fail to grow up in Christ. Let us look at a few of the characteristics of these persons.

• *The spiritually immature are repeatedly doing works of repentance.* My wife was reared in a church that often gave an invitation to come forward to a public altar and accept Christ. For some combination of reasons she had done this several times but still felt that something was lacking. When she was fourteen years old she responded one more time to the preacher's entreaty and went forward for prayer, but this time she said, "Lord, this is it. I want to be saved and I want to live for Jesus, but this is the last time I am doing this." She was a mature young woman and she was right; there was no

> ***Jesus encouraged each of us to be like a child in our faith but the scriptures warn us against childishness in our behavior. A child-like faith is mature but childish behavior is immature.***
>
> (Matt. 18:1-5, 1 Cor. 3:1-3, Heb. 6:1-3)

reason for her to repeatedly go to the altar to be saved or to receive any blessing that God has promised to those who will simply ask for it.

• *The spiritually immature contrive to remain the center of attention.* Churches appropriately give much attention to new converts. The testimony of the new convert is inspirational. Everyone wants to meet the new Christian. New Christians get many invitations to groups and events. After a few months, however, the new convert may no longer be the center of attention. Those who fail to grow may handle this by contriving to get the attention of the church.

During a special dedication service for a few persons in a local congregation, I observed the following incident. One man, accompanying a relative to the altar, immediately collapsed and fell to the floor, although rather softly clutching his friend on the way down. The pastor immediately moved to see what the problem was. Correctly discerning the situation the pastor said, "Our friend is fine and a medical doctor is present to help with any complications; let us continue with the service." Obviously not gaining the desired attention, the person who collapsed immediately jumped to his feet. The pastor had recognized his ploy and diffused his power to control. Of course most of us gain attention much more subtlely, but the intent is the same—keep me and my experience center stage. Some persons even choose to be a part of a nongrowing congregation so as to assure attention and a secure position in the group. Evangelism is sacrificed on the altar of immaturity.

• *The spiritually immature accept few if any responsibilities in the life of the church.* Even when they accept responsibilities, it is necessary to give an inordinate amount of attention to them for their work. Immature Christians may want the joy of being involved but they may not want to be responsible for any task.

• *The spiritually immature tend toward a carnal, rather than a humble and cooperative, spirit.* Carnal means the person is more like a sinner in attitude than like Christ. Explosive, bitter, overly critical, set on getting his or her own way, self-centered, and immoral may all describe carnal actions and attitudes. We can expect that new Christians may have some struggles with these actions and attitudes, but persons growing in Christ will increasingly bring these less-than-Christian attributes under control.

An unpleasant memory comes to my mind: some years ago a resource person for a ministers' meeting was discussing how sanctification is viewed by some as an instantaneous experience and by others as a process. One minister insisted strongly that sanctification was a one-time experience complete in itself. When it was evident that most ministers were not persuaded by his views, he arose and stomped out of the meeting announcing, "If you are not faithful to the truth then I want nothing to do with this meeting." The man was undoubtedly a deeply committed servant of the Lord, but he demonstrated an attitude that was far from the spirit of Christ.

Persons who continue to cling to carnal attitudes and actions remain babies in the Lord. They are saved by grace for eternity but they repeatedly make the here and now an unpleasant experience for the church. Probably few of us, if any, are totally innocent in these matters but a life-style of carnal attitudes and actions is childish.

WHAT DOES IT MEAN TO GROW UP?

In his commentary on Corinthians, Kenneth Chafin tells of a conference leader who asked each participant to take a pipe cleaner and shape a piece of art that symbolized his or her present spiritual condition. One man made a cradle and explained, "I'm a Christian who has never grown up so I thought this cradle best told the story" (1985, 52).

Growing up as a person is more than just getting older. Growing up as a disciple of Jesus Christ is more than just remaining in the church. Not too many years ago it was customary for local churches to have testimony meetings on Wednesday evenings at which time all those present would tell something of their present spiritual journey. Living the

> **Maturity is pressing toward the mark; immaturity is complacency and self-satisfaction.**
> —Roberta Hesteness (1988, 15)

Christian life was sometimes referred to as being "on the way" or "in the way." We laughed at the testimony of one person who announced, "I am pleased to witness that I have been saved and in the way for more than twenty years." The person was such an obstinate character that we put a different meaning to being "in the way" than he had intended. At least a few Christians have been more in the way than on the way.

Growing up is a *process*. Here are a few of the essential processes involved in growing up as a Christian—going on to maturity.

Growing up in *intellectual honesty*. It is a temptation to stay at a level where one seeks and accepts easy answers for complex problems. Not too many years ago a denominational leader provoked an outcry when he said that God would only hear the prayers of Christians. If one interprets a few verses rather literally, then it is possible to come to such a conclusion. The words of Jesus, "the Father will give you whatever you ask him in my name" (John 15:16) are not intended to suggest only Christians have a franchise on prayer. We are aware that God's conversations are much more inclusive than many of our theological systems.

In many critical situations we wish we could have a simple answer. Ron Sider, author of *Rich Christians,* has spoken helpfully to evangelicals about economic responsibility. In an appreciative review of Sider's thought, Tim Stafford suggested that Sider had seemed to say it is because of the economic sin of affluent nations that so many persons are hungry in under developed countries. Sider has reevaluated his position and recognized that poverty is much more complex and the answer to poverty is much more involved, demanding initiatives by leaders of both under developed and affluent countries (1992, 18-22).

On a more common and personal level we may repeatedly say, "Just pray about it," reducing prayer to some magic incantation. With such simplistic advice we ignore the fact that some action or confrontation may also be necessary.

More than one well-intentioned person has advised, "If you are having financial problems, then start tithing and that will solve all your difficulties." The truth is that money management is much more complex, and responsible handling of finances goes beyond tithing to a disciplined use all financial resources. Prayerful planning for all expenditures is a part of the discipline of tithing, but planning and discipline have to be a part of a total Christian stewardship of finances.

The most pervasive of all simple rationales is sometimes stated like this: "If we are all really Christian, then we will agree on this." For some reason we distort the biblical doctrine of unity to make it imperative that Christian persons agree on all matters. Of course it has never happened.

Growing up spiritually means learning to recognize the complexity of many of life's issues and getting past the easy answers so that some effective solutions can be found in personal, church, and community life.

Growing toward *positive thinking.* Positive thinking is not easy for many of us even with the help of Norman Vincent Peale, Robert Schuller, and Billy Graham. Truth is, Dr. Peale's wife and other associates have teased him about his own negative comments when he faces a speaking assignment.

Ruth Bell Graham confesses that family members often

called her husband Puddleglum, after a C. S. Lewis character, because of his tendency to see every possibility of something going wrong. She tells of a time that Bill was to stay in Miami and she was to proceed to their home in North Carolina. He learned the weather was bad in Atlanta, a stopover on her trip.

"You probably won't be able to land," he predicted. "If not, I don't know where you will go—probably on to New York City. But if they try to land, I hope you make it; Atlanta is one of the busiest airports in the United States. And if you do, I'd advise you to spend the night in a motel—if you can get a room, which I doubt—as a lot of planes will be grounded and the motels will be full. In that case, rent a car, if you can get one, and drive home. But drive carefully because ..."

You guessed it. "You could have a wreck!" (1982, 62-63). The experiences of these giants of the faith accent the discipline that is involved rather than give us an excuse for negative thinking.

An addiction to negative comments about the future, about the church, about other people, even about the world, inhibits spiritual growth. When I was a student at Anderson College, John A. Morrison was the president. A brilliant and practical man, he told us students more than once that there is a great difference between a critical mind, which he wanted for each of us, and a critical heart, which he warned would cripple us socially and spiritually.

A friend for whom I have a great deal of affection assured me several years ago that no one would walk on the moon. When the astronaut Neil Armstrong did just that, he assured me the government had conspired to make us believe someone had taken the walk. Another friend assured me the congregation which I pastored would never have a building fund campaign. When they voted to have the campaign, he let me know right away that I was going to be disappointed because no one would make a pledge. The day for commitments came and the goal was exceeded, but he informed me that the whole church was going to be in trouble because most of the people would never make good on their pledges.

81

> *Finally, beloved, whatever is true, whatever is honorable, whatever is just, whatever is pure, whatever is pleasing, whatever is commendable, if there is any excellence and if there is anything worthy of praise, think about these things.*
>
> —Philippians 4:8

A part of growing up spiritually is learning to think positively. For many of us a spiritual conversion experience is necessary for we have lived in homes and in churches that have practiced negative thinking so long that positive thinking is heresy.

Growing is *progress*. The statement seems redundant but too often we have heard of claims of growth by persons who were standing still. The Christian life is a pilgrimage.

Each year the Christian will
- learn something from experience
- learn something from other persons
- learn something from the Holy Spirit (John 14:26).

Christians are at different stages of learning and experiencing their faith. All Christians should be growing, going on to maturity. Even those Christians with an exemplary commitment and life-style are pilgrims. The Christian experience is a journey more than a destination, a process not a plateau, a life more than a concept. There is a "sacredness of your own journey," says Frederick Buechner (1982, 17).

Growing in the Lord involves an intentional progress in one's spiritual life. It is an adventure that includes some risks but one becomes stale when progress is not pursued.

Growing is *participation*. An essential part of personal spiritual development is close identification with other

Christians. That will include Christians with whom we may not totally agree. Acts 2:42-47 describes the daily meetings of the first Christians. A later group of Christ's followers were warned of the dangers of missing the worship services of the church (Heb. 10:24-25).

Isolation is a temptation
• when one is convinced others are not as committed
• when one has been hurt by an unkind word
• when business obligations pile up
• when one is not part of a decision-making group
• when worship styles are not comfortable
• when it is more convenient to have a personal time of worship or enjoy worship services on television
• when one has gotten out of the habit of going to church, due to illness or any one of several other excuses

Isolated Christians are not growing Christians because Christ created the church, in part, for the purpose of nurturing our faith. Participation in worship with other Christians is sometimes a difficult discipline but it is absolutely essential; it is not an option. Participation in small fellowship and prayer groups is an additional encouragement to growth.

Isolation breeds discontent and unfounded assumptions about what other people think and feel. Participation helps us understand other persons' views and creates a fellowship of pilgrims doing their very best to live for God.

A mature person is one who is using his or her spiritual gifts, who is building the body, who is discerning truth from error, who is speaking the truth in love, and who is in God-honoring relationships with people.
—Roberta Hesteness (1988, 14)

WHAT DOES IT MEAN TO BE MATURE?

Maturity is what we have been talking about throughout this book. Therefore, we can affirm that
- a mature Christian is humble, revering God and respecting persons
- a mature Christian is generous
- a mature Christian is accountable

Commitment and integrity are characteristic of a mature Christian. When humility, generosity, accountability, commitment, and integrity are identified as a set, three persons immediately come to my mind: Earl, Betty Jo, and Norm. I know each of them well but will mention one characteristic as a microcosm of each life.

Earl was a farmer when I best knew him, a farmer with one arm. He was a responsible church leader, able to speak and lead without demanding attention, often resisting leadership roles. When he led in prayer the words were simple but conveyed well the worship and petitions of the group. I never figured out how he managed to farm with his physical disadvantage but he was one of the best, and he was among the first to use modern mechanized and fertilizing methods in southeast Missouri. He was a member of the governing board for the Rural Electrification Association for years. Once when I mentioned to him and his wife, Izetta, that the lack of rain probably would result in a low farm yield he responded with a smile, "We will do all right. The Lord always seems to bless us with enough in spite of ourselves." He was just as positive about the church. His friend, O. C. Lewis, summed up Earl best: "He's all wool and a yard wide."

Betty Jo in no way resembles Earl except that she, too, is an exemplary mature Christian. A lay leader in the Meadow Park Church of God in Columbus, Ohio, she was my first choice as associate pastor when our young congregation recognized a need for additional personnel in leadership. She is intelligent, sensitive to other's hurts, and yet rather firm in stating and living her convictions; in other words, I never saw her get into a verbal scrap with anyone but do not recall her compromising anything she really believed to be essential. Betty Jo's maturity is best expressed in her continuing ability to speak affirming and reassuring words to so many persons. She has a way of zeroing in on a person's best personality or physical trait and mentioning it in a way that encourages. She makes a compliment seem like a revelation. She has a maturity that allows her to highlight the talents and gifts of other persons.

Norm is a capable lay minister of music, a faithful steward, and leader in several areas of church life. He is a public school principal but when I first met him he was constructing houses in Casper, Wyoming. He built a house for our family when we moved to the community. It was a fine home in many ways. Nearly a year after we had moved into our home another builder in our city had come to our home to obtain some information about the neighborhood. He asked who built our house. When I replied, "Norm did," he immediately said, "Then it is well built all the way through; that is the way Norm does it." Maturity is more a process than a plateau, as we have illustrated. Maturity is best described not by rationale but by stories from the lives of people. These three persons are among many who have demonstrated for me a maturity in the total scope of their Christian lives. In addition to their qualities of humility, generosity, and accountability, they are persons of deep commitment and integrity.

A mature Christian is committed. A spiritually mature person knows what he or she has decided about Christ and does not keep reconsidering decisions made long ago. The mature Christian can sing the traditional gospel song without any reservation:

I have decided to follow Jesus;
No turning back, no turning back.

The commitment made in younger years or as an adult has been tested repeatedly but no longer does the spiritually mature person question the decision to be a follower of Christ. The decision has been made.

In the milieu of experience this commitment has resulted in a "stick-to-it-tiveness." Mature Christians are known by their discipline of following through on their assignments in the life of the church and the community. Their word is their bond but they rarely say that; they do as they have indicated they will do. Mature Christians are persistent in their faith.

Mature Christians have integrity. In addition to being persistent they are consistent. What they believe finds expression in their family, church, and community life. Honesty and morality are lived out, not just talked about. They practice what they preach, live out what they believe. They do not try to change biblical teachings by rationalization. Sexual morality is binding. A compassionate morality for suffering persons repeatedly emerges, though at times discomforting and disruptive. Mature Christians consistently realign their lives through reference to the Holy Word and by a repeated comparison of their spirits with the Spirit of Christ.

FOR MEDITATION OR DISCUSSION

1. Place a check mark (✓) beside those attitudes or actions that best describe your present level of Christian living. *Remember that new Christians are not expected to be mature.* Remember also that even persons who have served Christ for many years may need to correct an immature attitude or set of actions.

IMMATURE
- Repeatedly repenting same sins, beginning over
- Continued need of special, individual attention
- Not responsibly involved in life of church
- Carnal, combative attitude; not cooperative
- I am a recent convert, a new Christian

What other attitudes and actions indicate immaturity in the life of a disciple of Christ?

GROWING UP
- Seeks honest answers to serious questions; no simplistic answers
- Learning to think positively
- Progressing in the faith, doing better than before
- Participating in the fellowship with many other Christians

What other attitudes or disciplines may indicate one is growing as a disciple of Christ?

MATURE
- Reverence for God
- Respect for other persons
- Generous with time and finances and in relationships
- Personally accountable to other Christians
- Committed: decisions have been made with out waffling on Christ or his church
- Integrity: the way I live is consistent with what I believe and claim to live as a Christian

What are some other indicators of Christian maturity?

2. Which factors in the life of a new Christian do you think most often hinder spiritual growth? Rate the following:(**a:** will indicate that which is a factor most often; **b:** the second most often, and so forth.
___ Family of birth has non-Christian habits
___ Cultural values are different from that of a Christian
___ Enslavement to a particular sin; conversion in some aspects of life takes time
___ The life-style of many church members discourages a new convert
___ Other:

3. What factors best help a person grow as a Christian?
- Support of family   • Friends who are Christians
- Enthusiastic church • A pattern of instruction
- Depends solely on person
- Other:

7

Enabling Spiritual Experiences

Roberta is a Christian who lives for Christ about as well as anyone I know. She is pious in the best sense of that word, generous with her more-than-average wealth, and a faithful church member, both in worship and work. She surprised me when she said in a class session, "Pastor, I don't know exactly when I was saved. I grew up in a Christian home, and it seems that as early as I can remember I knew who Jesus was and that he was my Savior and Lord." Roberta had affirmed the personal information given by others about when they had accepted Christ, but her own experience was not so easily dated and described.

Donald and Tamara presented their daughter Hannah in a parent-child dedication during a Sunday morning worship. Pastor Johnson said, "This is church growth at its best." I affirmed his comment, for rearing children in the path they should go is the best evangelism plan I know. Hannah may well give the same testimony as Roberta in years to come, or she may recall a time early in her childhood or youth that she consciously received Christ's forgiveness for her sins.

Christian experiences are similar but they do not all fit easily into the same box, the same "how to" outline. A variety of religious experiences—all of them transforming and real—are part of the holiness and evangelical tradition I have known.

> *At last, meditating day and night and by the mercy of God, I ... began to understand that the righteousness of God is that through which the righteous live by a gift of God, namely faith. . . . Here I felt as if I were entirely born again and had entered paradise itself through gates that had been flung open.*
>
> —Martin Luther (15)

High-quality Christians are known to consistently report common spiritual experiences that seem to be integral to living the high quality Christian life. It appears that those who ignore these experiences or undervalue them have a less effective witness for Christ and his church, perhaps a less transforming and enjoyable experience of their faith.

SPIRITUAL EXPERIENCES

Two spiritual experiences are critical in the life of exemplary Christians and are once-in-a-lifetime happenings. Three other spiritual experiences are common to these persons, sometimes repeated a few times, and usually result in a greater sense of trust and commitment. No questionnaires or other types of systematic studies have been undertaken to prove the point. Rather, these experiences in some form or another have been brought to light by observation and conversation.

The two critical spiritual experiences are salvation and sanctification. The other three types of experiences may be summarized by these labels: euphoria, course correction, and ultimate meaning.

SALVATION

Many speak of a spiritual awareness or awakening that preceded any type of decision for Christ. This awareness can come at any point and at any age. Barbara Miller amazed me during her missionary candidate interview when she explained that she first felt her call to be a missionary when she was four years old. I do not recall any awareness of spiritual things on a personal level until I was at least twelve years old. Ralph, another friend, who started regularly attending church as an adult, told me that he had never even thought of the spiritual side of his life until he was in his twenties.

For some, spiritual awareness or awakening came in the day-to-day life of a Christian family. For others it first appeared during instruction in the catechism. Still others gradually realized over a period of years a spiritual nature that was more than their physical body or their mental nature. Some became acutely aware of guilt as they first heard or read the gospel.

> *This is the message we have heard from him and proclaim to you, that God is light and in him there is no darkness at all. If we say that we have fellowship with him while we are walking in darkness, we lie and do not what is true; but if we walk in the light as he himself is in the light, we have fellowship with one another, and the blood of Jesus his Son cleanses us from all sin. If we say that we have no sin, we deceive ourselves, and the truth is not in us. If we confess our sins, he who is faithful and just will forgive us our sins and cleanse us from all unrighteousness.*
>
> *—1 John 1:5-9*

By whatever process, most exemplary Christians, at a specific time, prayed for forgiveness of sins and promised to live for Jesus Christ. The definitive salvation experience has occurred in a variety of ways:

- For many it came in a quiet meditative moment alone.
- Some responded to a sermon or a worship service.
- Many others, in the depths of conviction for a sinful life, emotionally asked God's forgiveness and accepted salvation.
- Still others recall a time they personally confirmed Christ as Lord of their lives.

Alice was not able to put a date on such an experience but she did say, "I know somewhere along the way I made that commitment and I have known I was saved all along." She would warn of the dangers of pretending salvation when in reality salvation has never been accepted. She, and the gospel message, encourage a time of decision about a life of sin and the life of salvation. By whatever process persons came to Christ, they all can sing with fervor

I once was lost but now am found,
Was blind but now I see.

Gloria Gaither, gospel song lyricist and member of the famous Gaither Trio, gives yet another perspective on the experience of salvation in Christ. She writes:

I am learning life is a process. Even my very salvation is a process. True, it began years ago with a choice, but even my choosing then was embryonic. At first, I chose "in part" because "part" was all I knew. But as my choices have been confirmed by His trustworthiness, I have become a bigger risker for His sake. Indeed, I am coming to know that, paradoxically, risky living is the only safe way to go (1988, 9).

When persons speak of their salvation in Christ, a remarkable bouquet of experiences are reported. We sense loss when these experiences are forced into one form and the spice of

> *In one morning service, standing with her dad and singing an invitation hymn, she thought she was the worst sinner who had ever been created [Lillie Sowers (McCutcheon), age seven]. Across her mind flashed the painful memory of when she secretly had stolen a candy bar. . . .*
>
> *Lillie longed for forgiveness. She asked her father if she were allowed to go to the altar. "A big old salty tear dropped off his boney check down to his feet," recalled Lillie. His only response was, "Yes, Lillie Bud!" So to the altar she went after another verse or two, with her father's great big arm around her. . . . Her sin was swallowed up in forgiveness. She was protected and guided by God's powerful arm, always glad for herself to be hidden behind the shadow of the cross of God's Son.*
> —Barry L. Callen (1992, 47-48)

variety is lost to the church. Just as persons relate to one another in a multitude of unique ways, even persons who are twins, so does each of us experience God in different ways. The essence of salvation is defined by the scriptures but our experience is the reality. The high quality Christian is able to say, "I know I have been forgiven and Christ is Lord of my life." For most it is an identifiable moment of decision; for a few it is something that happened but no precise turning point can be identified either on the calendar or geographically.

SANCTIFICATION

In my Christian tradition we have identified sanctification as a second definite work of grace, salvation being the first. Perhaps too simply we could say that salvation is forgiveness by the grace of God and sanctification is cleansing of the Christian for service to God. It is not my purpose here to debate the merits of that view of sanctification.

Five aspects of sanctification on which many Christians agree are the following:
(1) Sanctification is the work of the Holy Spirit in the life of the believer.
(2) Sanctification means a person is set aside for God's purposes, such as utensils were set aside for use in worship in the temple. (You may want to read again in Daniel 5 how Nebuchadnezzar got into trouble by using these utensils for purposes other than worship.)
(3) Sanctification often includes an experience of calling to a vocation or to a high purpose.
(4) Sanctification includes a commitment to the leadership of the Holy Spirit and anticipates guidance in many decisions, large and small.
(5) Sanctification is a commitment to the guidance of the Holy Spirit in one's life.

Christians disagree on this subject in at least two ways:
(1) Many believe that one is sanctified—purified—at the time of salvation; some believe God cleanses the believer when the Christian makes a full surrender of his or her life; another group believes sanctification is a gradual process of growth in the Lord; and a fourth group believes that Christians are ultimately sanctified at the end of the age when they stand before the Lord. Most Christians who believe in a sanctified life believe that it involves a process of growth, however it begins.
(2) Charismatics tend to believe the evidence of the experience of the Holy Spirit is speaking in tongues; holiness or

Wesleyan groups believe the evidence is a holy life; others say there is no witness until one has completed a faithful life of service and that alone is the convincing witness.

Knowing the wide range of interpretations of the scriptures and the theology on this subject, I am aware many will take exception to the way I have outlined the similarities and differences. The whole list of comparisons is for the purpose of making this one statement. *Persons who live a high quality Christian life often speak of an experience with God when their hearts and lives were set aside totally for his will and his way.*

OTHER SPIRITUAL EXPERIENCES

Mature Christians often tell of at least three other spiritual experiences: *euphoria, course correction, and ultimate meaning.*

It must be repeated here:

- No set pattern exists for these experiences from person to person.
- A wide variety of significant worship and other types of encounters with God are reported by Christians, in addition to the ones listed.

1. *Euphoria.* Many Christians recall unpremeditated and unexpected times when the Spirit of God ministered to them with a feeling of encouragement and, on a few occasions, with specific information. I recall a holiday when I was driving from my home to a nearby super market. At the intersection of Indiana Routes 32 and 109, as I waited on a traffic light to change, I felt the calm deep assurance of God that sent a warm sensation throughout my body. My life was richer and more confident than before that moment. The content of the experience was God's Spirit in me; no conceptual information was provided.

2. *Course Correction.* Nearly all persons who have lived the Christian life for a few years speak of times when they

> *Suddenly the ground seemed to give way beneath me, and I found myself in quite another region. Within five minutes I went through some such reflections as the following: the loneliness of the human soul is unendurable; nothing can penetrate it except the highest intensity of that sort of love that the religious teachers have preached; whatever does not spring from this motive is harmful, or at best useless; . . . . At the end of those five minutes, I had become a completely different person. For a time, a sort of mystic illumination possessed me.*
>
> —Bertrand Russell (Kimball 1992)

realized some changes had to be made in their lives. Perhaps wrong, or at least inappropriate, choices had been made. The course correction may have meant that an apology had to be spoken or written and blame had to be accepted without reservation. Some have spoken of times of participating in forgiveness—that is, forgiving and accepting forgiveness. Many have told of making the wrong decision about a place to live, or the direction of educational programs and even vocational choices. A typical confession might be, "God finally got through to me and I realized I had to go a different direction with my life, if I were going to be a Christian."

3. *Ultimate meaning.* For the most part, I have observed this experience or had it reported by persons fifty-five years of age or older, or by persons who have been told they have an incurable disease that may soon take their life. It is an experience of ultimate meaning, when they say, "my life has meaning beyond anything that is here and now." Many Christians experience this as faith and hope. These persons seem to

experience on earth a portion of that which shall be experienced in total when we are with God in eternity.

It is an *acceptance* of life as it is without protest.

It is a *satisfaction* that life as we know it is finished and that is not bad.

It is an *amen* to all that God has done and will do.

It is a *conclusion* "I am ready and I totally trust God."

I asked Sister Sawyers just before I left her apartment if I could voice our prayer together. She said that she wanted me to know something first. Her doctor had told her that she probably would not live more than six months. She did not want to worry her children about her health, but she was planning to visit them and let them know of her condition. She said, "Do not pray for the Lord to heal me; he has done that many times. I have lived a good life. I am alone now except for occasional visits. If I live it will be with serious health problems. I am ready to be with the Lord." I honored her request not to mention our conversation to anyone and simply prayed for her comfort and good visits with her family. She died about eight months later. She had experienced the ultimate in meaning for her life and had no protest.

FOR MEDITATION OR DISCUSSION

An observation: A few spiritual experiences are commonly reported by Christians and these experiences seem to be integral to living the high quality Christian life. Do you think that those who ignore these experiences or undervalue them have a less effective witness for Christ and his church and a less transforming and enjoyable experience of their faith?

1. *Salvation* (saved, born again, accepted Christ as Savior and Lord): by whatever process, many persons have, at specific times, prayed for forgiveness of sins and promised to live for Jesus Christ (John 3:1-10; Acts 2:35; Romans 3:22-24). Check the statements that apply to you.

__ I remember the age, or event, when I became spiritually aware or had an awakening.

__ I know when I was saved:

date _____

place _____

__ I have known about Jesus as long as I can remember and have always believed him to be my Savior and Lord.

__I have never accepted Christ as Savior and Lord.

__Other:

2. Sanctification: In some fellowships sanctification is taught as a second definite work of grace. Many Christians agree that sanctification is the work of the Holy Spirit in the believer. It means a person is set aside for God's purposes, often involves a call to vocation or high purpose, and includes a commitment to the leadership of the Holy Spirit (Acts 1:8, 2:1-4, 9:17, 10:44, 19:6; 1 Thessalonians 4:3-4; Romans 12:1; Ezekiel 42; Daniel 5).

__ I have had an experience of sanctification that took place at a specific time in my life.

__ Sanctification has been a growth process for me and has not included a specific event.

__ I have experienced both an event of sanctification and sanctification as a growth process.

__ Sanctification has been for me an awareness of the Spirit's power and call on my life.

__ Sanctification is a purified state I will achieve only at the end of my life, through the grace of God.

__ Other:

3. *Euphoria:* Many Christians recall one or a few unpremeditated and unexpected times when the Spirit of God ministered to them with a feeling of encouragement and, on a few occasions, with specific information. The content of the experience is an inner awareness of God's Spirit and the information is more realization than conceptual information (2 Cor. 12:1-4).

__ I have had a euphoric spiritual experience.

__ I do not recall ever having this type of experience.

__ I have no understanding of the euphoric experience.

__ Other:

4. *Course Correction:* Many Christians speak of times when it became obvious that changes had to be made in attitudes, habits, or actions. One said, "God finally got through to me and I realized my attitudes and the direction of my life had to be different." Another, "It was painfully clear to me that I had to go back and apologize, if I were to live for Christ." Another, "I knew my habits had to change" (Acts 11:4-18).

   __ I have made course corrections as a result of very definite spiritual experiences or inspiration.

   __ I do not recall any time I have made course corrections for spiritual reasons; my course changes have been more the result of logic or for social reasons.

   __ Other:

5. *Ultimate fulfillment/meaning:* Some Christians have reported an experience of ultimate fulfillment or meaning, a deep assurance that his or her eternal life has meaning beyond anything here and now. (Most Christians experience this by faith—a hint of what we shall know when we are with God in eternity.) It is an acceptance of life as it is without protest. It is an Amen to all that God has done and will do. It is an absolute personal trust in God. Many Christians have expressed this kind of faith near death; others have spoken of a sense of fulfillment—"I have fought the good fight, I have finished the race, I have kept the faith" (2 Tim. 4:7).

   __ I have experienced a deep sense of ultimate fulfillment that has significantly elevated the quality of my life.

   __ I do not know that I have had such an experience.

   __Other:

8

Hi-C Churches

I recall a riddle from childhood: A farmer came to a stream carrying with him three items: a sack of grain, a chicken, and a fox. The boat was large enough for the farmer to transport only himself and one of his possessions at a time. He would have to make three trips to get his group across the stream but this created a problem. If he left the chicken with the fox on either side of the stream, the chicken would be eaten. If he left the chicken with the grain on either side, the chicken would eat the grain. How did the farmer get himself and the three items across the stream?

The answer: First he transported the chicken over the stream and left it on the far side. He returned and picked up the grain, transported it to the far shore, and picked up the chicken and took it back with him. The farmer left the chicken and took the fox to the far shore and left the fox with the grain; then he returned for the chicken. Thus he never left the fox to eat the chicken or the chicken to eat the grain.

Many congregations are trying to solve a different kind of riddle in our day, one posed by this question: How can we be a growing congregation and at the same time be a church that insists on a high commitment to discipleship?

Many are convinced it cannot be done. Several are seeking to learn how to do it. A few are doing both: they are experiencing exceptional growth and practicing serious discipleship.

COMMITMENT MAKES THE DIFFERENCE

Lyle Schaller, church consultant and writer, has said that an essential part of a growing church is the demand for high commitment. Schaller has guided more than three thousand congregations through a self analysis enabling them to consider the alternatives for their future ministry. Fifty representatives of more than twenty church groups in the United States met with him in Richmond, Indiana, to learn from the master consultant. The second day Lyle asked each of us to state why we were attending the conference.

I said, "My church group has had a decline in Sunday morning worship and Sunday school attendance during the 80s. The past two years we have seen a slight increase in attendance. I want to know how to keep our church in the United States growing."

Schaller surprised me by saying, "I don't have to wait to answer your question. I can tell you now for I know your group well. You have been a high commitment group and when you become a high commitment church again you will grow."

> *The most common way to judge the health of Christianity is to examine the vitality of local churches. The most visible impact of the faith is seen at the congregational level. It is through the corporate practice of the faith that observers gain their clearest notion of what the Christian faith is about. And through the practice of Christianity in the congregational context, believers receive their greatest encouragement, edification and equipping for continued personal growth and ministry.*
> —George Barna (1990, 130)

He reminded us that Dean Kelley's book may have been, as Kelley suggests, more accurately called "Why Strict Churches Are Strong," conservative or liberal, rather than *Why Conservative Churches Are Growing* (Kelly 1986, XVII-XVIII).

Hi-C churches, high commitment congregations, are essential if we are to see in this and the next generation Hi-Q Christians, high-quality disciples of Christ, who make a significant difference in their families, communities, schools, jobs, and churches.

Church growth that only increases the number of sick, morally compromising, or casual Christians is really not worth the effort. Church growth that develops responsible, courageous, and committed disciples is desperately needed in this decade and the beginning of the next century.

A couple of generations of church leaders have expressed the fear that a strict approach will chase away members and be perceived as self-righteous. Persons in the present generation, however, who are taking the faith seriously appear to be responding to churches that demand specific and well defined commitments. The likes of Lyle Schaller, George Barna, and Dean Kelley, among other church analysts, agree that haphazardly run, routinely operated, "pay attention to the words not the music" type churches do not have much of a chance to succeed.

My Dad first told me the story of a mountaineer sitting on his porch. A young neighbor came walking down the road beside the creek. The man on the porch yelled. "Sorry to hear about your pa."

The walking one answered, "Yeah, we were surprised."

The man on the porch continued, "What did he die of?"

The young man said, "I don't rightly remember, but I remember it was nothing serious."

Thousands of churches are dying, most of them of nothing serious, as far as we can tell. A clue can be found to their ailment when we discover that many churches are failing to ask for high quality lives from their members.

THE HIGH COMMITMENT CHURCH

1. MEMBERSHIP IS ON THE BASIS OF A COVENANT IN A HIGH COMMITMENT CHURCH.

2. MISSION IS THE PURPOSE OF A HIGH COMMITMENT CHURCH.

3. MINISTRY IS THE VOCATION OF THE MEMBERS OF A HIGH COMMITMENT CHURCH.

4. MORALITY IS THE STANDARD IN A HIGH COMMITMENT CHURCH.

5. LEADERSHIP IS SPECIAL IN A HIGH COMMITMENT CHURCH.

6. SPIRITUALITY IS OPENLY DISCUSSED, SOUGHT, AND ENCOURAGED IN A HIGH COMMITMENT CHURCH.

CHARACTERISTICS OF A
HIGH-COMMITMENT CHURCH

Covenant Membership

Membership is on the basis of a covenant in a high commitment church. The covenant is not necessarily written but it is understood from the beginning of a person's membership. He or she can expect some benefits from the fellowship in exchange for specific commitments from each member. Covenant membership means an obvious mutuality in ministry to and with each other.

Everyone is welcome to worship and participate in the education and program of the church. Membership is something special and persons are not encouraged to claim membership without pledging responsibility in the group.

105

The congregation in which I learned the faith did not have a membership roll or a written creed. Even so, we knew who were the members and who were not. Though a growing church, no effort was made to make people feel as though they were members if they had not made a personal commitment to Christ and his people.

We were expected to be present for worship services and testify, however briefly, in Wednesday evening prayer meeting. We could not attend movies, smoke, drink alcoholic beverages, or dance. A few of these expectations and prohibitions may be naive in our day, but they were a part of the basis of covenant in our church. Our church was at once the most demanding yet the fastest growing church in the city.

In return we were promised fun, acceptance as an important person, God's blessing on our lives, prayer for us when we needed it, help in time of trouble, and a divine call on each of our lives. Most of the young people felt that the covenant, though an informal one, was quite a bargain.

Our present generation, I think, would request a broader covenant and one less focused on the "shall nots." Nonetheless, local churches serve best who are able to clearly state to prospective members exactly what to expect and what is expected.

A pastor's class was the place and time we shared the covenant concept when I served in Casper, Wyoming. The Sunday school hour provided an opportunity for twelve sessions led by an associate pastor for new converts and members new to the fellowship. In addition, I led a fast-paced three-hour session on the third Saturday morning of each month.

Two concerns repeatedly emerged for the groups I led and for me as the pastor: What do you mean when you ask us if we are Christian? What is the financial obligation of a member?

I eventually arrived at two simple answers that satisfied both the needs of the local church and the needs of the potential new members:

Concerning salvation: Have you confessed your sins to

Christ, asked forgiveness, and promised to live for Christ the rest of your life? That is the biblical meaning of being born again, of conversion, of what it means to begin to be a disciple. Church membership, baptism, and previous acceptance by a group are appreciated but meaningless unless founded on a personal acceptance of Christ as both Savior and Lord.

I then invited any persons who had not made that type of commitment to stay after the class session if they would like to talk further about their relationship with Christ. Following every session at least one person stayed and prayed for forgiveness and committed to serve the Lord.

Concerning money: As thoughtfully and thoroughly as time allowed, I explained that the church operated totally on the offerings given by members of the church and that no national group or wealthy individual took care of our financial obligations for programs, salaries, buildings, or missions. Then I said something which I would never have said earlier in my ministry: "We would love to have you as a member of our congregation. However, if you do not intend to give a regular significant offering based on your income you will probably be happier in another church. Frankly, we just do not need more persons who will not accept the challenge of stewardship. Financial costs are involved in many of the things we believe God is calling us to do and we are looking for members who are willing to commit themselves and a portion of their finances to fulfill our mission."

I assured the group that anyone was welcome to worship with us and take advantage of our ministries but calling oneself a member meant acceptance of major obligations. Not one person ever objected to that standard and every family picked up offering envelopes, available on a display table. That's the way, I believe strongly, it should be.

Purpose: Mission

Mission is the purpose of a high commitment church. The purposes of the church are several: worship, discipleship, evangelism, fellowship, ministry to each other, and the like. The church is also a task force on mission for Christ in the

WHAT YOU CAN EXPECT FROM THE CHURCH

• *The word of God proclaimed and taught in understandable language, relevant to your life, in the context of celebrative worship.*

• *The ordinances (sacraments) administered with dignity.*

• *A challenge and opportunity to equip yourself for ministry both within the fellowship and to the community.*

• *Prayer for you, especially in times of special need such as illness, decisions, success, and failure.*

• *Guidance for life, including instructions for life from the pulpit and personal counseling when requested.*

• *An awareness of and response to your basic human needs, including housing, clothing, health, and education but also your need for compassion, understanding, and challenge.*

• *Inclusion in meaningful fellowships, both large and small, within the church.*

• *Friendship.*

WHAT YOUR CHURCH EXPECTS FROM YOU

• *Regular participation in the church's worship services.*

• *Commitment to grow in Christ, to change, to be a spiritual person in the community.*

• *A caring ministry to other members of the fellowship, in keeping with your recognized gifts and talents.*

• *Participation in the mission of the church to the local and world communities, with prayers, volunteer work, and gifts.*

• *Systematic and significant financial offerings to sustain and expand the ministry and mission of the local church.*

• *Prayer for the pastor and lay leaders coupled with a commitment to speak positively about your church.*

• *Friendship.*

community. The high commitment church is involved in what has been categorized as social work; it must be on mission in order to carry out Christ's instructions. Social work, however, does not take the place of evangelism or personal piety. Hi-C churches that give due attention to the basics of the faith tend to be more effective in their social ministries.

Hillary Clinton has been active in ministries to children and in lobbying for the interests of abused and neglected children. The First Lady, a member of the Methodist Church, has been open and frank in statements about her faith, both in the secular and religious press. She says Methodism's "emphasis on personal salvation combined with active applied Christianity" is a "practical method of trying to live as a Christian in a difficult and challenging world" (Cornell 1982, 63). Mrs. Clinton recalls that her church youth group ministered to children of Mexican migrant workers picking crops near her home and to children of poverty in the city and says, "What my church taught me is, because I had those blessings from the family, I owed something back. . . . And for me that took the shape early on in caring about children (Anthony 1992,98).

Mission service to the community means that the local church opens its eyes to human needs. Two congregations with which I am acquainted have a Seeing Committee of three persons. It is their responsibility to keep their eyes and ears open to individual and family needs in the church and in the community and to marshal persons and materials to meet those needs through volunteer service and contributions of needed items. One of the committee members has washing machines, refrigerators, toys, and miscellaneous other items in his garage, ready to respond to needs. They have often enlisted several persons to help a single mother move her family to a new residence, for instance.

The Community Service Workers of Wichita's Central Community Church meets on the first Saturday of each month for a breakfast, and then workers depart to various sites throughout the city to paint, roof, rake leaves, cut down trees, help people move, and even clean house. The services are focused on the needs of older and single persons.

LOAVES, FISHES, AND BICYCLES

Caryn began tutoring a young Hispanic boy in Guadalupe, a Latino neighborhood near Phoenix. She learned he wanted a bicycle and she wanted to provide it, but was sure the other five children in the family would be disappointed when they saw only one bicycle. She delivered the gift to her student and she was correct; the disappointment showed on the children's faces.

She asked her pastor if any funds could be made available from the Faith Promise Missions Budget to purchase four bikes. He agreed, but on second thought suggested he would just ask the congregation if any had a bicycle they could give for the youngsters. The need was announced in the next worship service. Following the service nine-year-old Eric told his parents that he wanted to give his new bicycle, still in its box, to the Hispanic children. His parents were surprised at Eric's generosity, but agreed to let him make the gift. They told the pastor.

At the next worship service the pastor announced what Eric had done. At the end of the service forty-three bicycles had been given for the children in Guadalupe; the bicycle gifts grew to sixty-three in a few days. A member said to the pastor, "If you have any need for help with the bicycles call this man," and gave him a name. The pastor did not take the offer too seriously but in courtesy called the man a few days later. The man informed the pastor that he was a retired lieutenant colonel and invited the pastor over to see his shop. More than two hundred bicycles hung about in various states of repair. The retired officer said that he repaired bikes and gave them to Guadalupe children and other children in poverty.

The pastor asked the gentleman to come to church the next Sunday and tell the congregation about his work. Though not Christians, the man and his wife came and he briefly explained what he was doing with bicycles. At the conclusion of the pastor's sermon both he and his wife were so moved by the service that they committed their lives to Christ.

That is the story of the bicycles. You can read about the loaves and fishes in the New Testament, John 6:1-13.

—O.W.

111

The local church is on mission to the world. During the presidential campaign at the end of the thirties, candidate Wendell Willkie spoke of One World. In more recent years many have spoken of a world economy, and a world market. The local church has always had a world concept in reference to missions. No city, state, national, or continental boundaries inhibit the concern of the church that Christ established. The spiritual condition of all persons is a prayerful concern for the church. The Christian fellowship does not erase from its consciousness the faces of starving children, the uneducated masses, or those under military and political bondage.

The church that is really God's church, Christ's church, the church in which the Holy Spirit dwells and empowers is on a mission in the whole world. Though not called as individuals or as a group to go to all nations, the local church seeks ways to pray for, encourage, and support those who do have and accept the call. The Hi-C church is on a world mission.

In more than twenty-five years of pastoring I have never seen the time when local building, personnel, and program needs did not demand more than the financial resources available. In all those years never was there one day when world needs were not pressing—the starving, the imprisoned, the betrayed. The churches I have pastored, without exception, had lay leadership who insisted that local needs would be met but not by compromising our involvement in world missions. One year we had just completed a capital funds campaign to which more than five hundred thousand dollars had been committed over a three-year period. I was convinced this would not be a good year for a missions convention. With the encouragement of lay leaders, we had the convention and received Faith Promise commitments totaling nearly fifty thousand dollars. I knew that some were communicating to me that if there were a choice between giving to missions or to the new building, missions would come first. I heard and applauded their world consciousness.

Evangelism is at the heart of what the church is all about. Whatever the methods—and there are several good ones—the Hi-C church is about the marvelous task of calling persons to

I've fly fished for thirty years at least. I belong to three different fly fishing clubs, receive three different magazines on fly fishing, and three newsletters. Over the years I have personally introduced fifteen people to fly fishing. I know because at home I have a little publication, "To Cast a Fly," and on the inside cover I keep a running list of everyone I have gotten involved in fly fishing. Now, if I am that enthusiastic about fly fishing as a sport, shouldn't I be even more enthusiastic about introducing someone to Jesus Christ?

Fred Dunwiddie (1991)

Christ Jesus. Whatever good the church may do, if it fails to persuade persons to accept salvation and make Christ their Lord, in a great measure it fails to be the church.

Members in Ministry

Ministry is the vocation of the members of a high commitment church. It sounds like a cliché but a sign in a church I visited expresses the idea: "Every member is a minister." A characteristic of a Hi-C Church is people who are concerned about each other and help each other. A characteristic of a preoccupied group of people who worship together is an ignorance of each other's interests and feelings.

Spiritual gifts are continuing to be rediscovered by local churches. Dozens of books have been written on the discovery and use of gifts. Spiritual-gifts workbooks and personal inventories are available from most denominational offices. The truth rediscovered is this: God endows every member of the church in a special way(s) that enables that person to minister to other members. An ongoing and demanding task of any

> **Beloved, since God loved us so much, we also ought to love one another. No one has ever seen God; if we love one another, God lives in us, and his love is perfected in us . . . . The commandment we have from him is this: those who love God must love their brothers and sisters also.**
>
> —1 John 4:11-12, 21

local church is challenging and training members of the church to use their spiritual gifts. Of course, many pastors and lay leaders have long recognized the other side of that coin: discovering kind ways to discourage members who tend to exercise gifts they do not have.

Some groups do not recognize a group as a local congregation until, among other things, all the biblical gifts are present in the fellowship. The discovery and exercise of spiritual gifts by members is a part of being a Hi-C Church.

A close and concerned relationship with a few is a part of each member's responsibility. None can be involved with everyone, even in a small church of fifty members, but all can be involved with eight or ten persons who pray for each other regularly and serve each other in times of personal need. The emergence of Small Group Ministries, Koinonia Groups, Twelve-Step Groups, or Cell Groups in thousands of churches has helped produce a personalized ministry in a world of lonely people.

A few in every church group will require a ministry focused on them—that is, the church will always have some who are a mission in themselves. Their salaries may always be inadequate and unwisely used, the habits of some family members may be destructive to others, some seem to have recurring emergencies, and sometimes new converts have life-styles and situations that require all the special attention other members can give to help them get a new start in life.

Generosity is needed by every one in the church. In a previous chapter we have spoken at length about generosity. It is possible for the word to be used only in relation to financial gifts. Just as important is a generous attitude to all worshipers. A smile, an openness, a handshake, an attempt to learn and remember names, a pause for conversation, intentional compliments, inquiry about family members or a recent vacation

---

PEOPLE AS LEGOS?

Do you know what Legos look like? They are pieces of plastic that can be snapped together into creatively designed toys. Children love them. Legos can be made into cars, stores, bridges, houses, schools, and church buildings. Most Legos have about six snap-on points. Some have many more, and a few have only two or four. When a Lego is all snapped up, you simply can't attach anything more to it. The only way to snap on something new is to unsnap something old.

The social structure of churches is made up of people like Legos. They have a limited number of snap-on points—few have more than six. After people have been in a church for a couple of years, they are all snapped up. . . .

So what should a church do? Seek to snap newcomers to newcomers. Most of them have several snap-on points available and are looking for relationships.

—Leith Anderson (1992, 136)

---

experience, and many other thoughtful words and actions toward other members is a part of what it is to be a member in ministry. Hi-C churches are bubbly; the sound you hear before and after services is the sound of mutual concern.

Morality

Morality is the standard in a high commitment church. Biblical morality is defined well in Galatians. It may at first seem redundant to insist that Christians live moral lives. In our age, as in that of Paul, some believed sexual morality to be a matter of personal business and of no concern to the church. Our point is not that the church's only concern with morality is a focus on sexual morality. Nor do we attempt to provide an answer to the complex sexual morality questions present in today's church. The point is that morality is a major concern for a Hi-C church and sexual morality is a specific concern increasingly faced by local churches.

A minister for singles in a local church expressed a frustration that many persons of her group saw no harm in single Christians having sexual intercourse with friends, particularly if they were previously married. A lay person in a denominational planning group was in tears as she expressed dismay over the fact that married persons generally known to be involved in illicit relationships were not being asked to relinquish leadership in her church. Perhaps these are isolated occurrences, but many persons feel that sexual activity is none of the church's business and any mention of it is, at best, quaint and naive.

> *Gallup reports the most bewildering paradox: religion up, morality down. . . .*
>
> *Looking at the state of evangelicalism and the state of the culture gives little room for optimism: How can we expect others to take what we profess to believe more seriously than we ourselves apparently do?*
>
> —Charles Colson (1992)

> *Therefore, friends, select from among your-selves seven men of good standing, full of the Spirit and of wisdom, whom we may appoint to this task, while we, for our part, will devote our-selves to prayer and to serving the word.*
> —Acts 6:3-4

High-commitment churches let it be known from the pulpit, in classrooms, and in printed materials that members are expected to experience intimate sexual relationships only in the context of marriage. It is difficult to see how a church committed to biblical teachings can expect anything else from its members.

Divorce is not taken casually in a Hi-C church. One lay leader commented, "In our congregation we essentially tend to isolate persons who are getting a divorce but if someone moves into our congregation who has been divorced or has divorced and remarried we feel their previous problems are not our concern. I don't have any ideas about how to do it differently but that seems like a double standard to me."

A pastor said, "I am aware of all of our statements on procedure but members who get a divorce continue to be a perplexing practical problem for me. I want to help both parties during a crucial time of failure and injury and I know that seldom is there a totally innocent party in a divorce, but on what basis do persons participate as members and on what basis are they excluded?" Another pastor acknowledged that as many as half of the members of his conservative and evangelical church had been divorced.

A commonly held conclusion in our Western culture is that divorce is a personal matter and has little to do with personal morality. Even in Christian circles this is becoming the commonly accepted standard. It is difficult to understand how a church based on biblical teachings can accept divorce as simply a personal matter.

A Hi-C church will
• make known in a variety of ways the sacredness and permanence of the marriage vows
• provide marriage enrichment programs and clinics
• structure programs to serve persons suffering through and recovering from divorce

The high-commitment church will also
• reserve and exercise the right to request that persons going through divorce not serve in conspicuous leadership and up front worship roles for a period of time
• expect Christian behavior on the part of all members including divorcing or recently divorced persons in courtship and other relationships.

Divorcing persons are needy and vulnerable. Many divorcing and divorced persons are deeply committed Christians and many of them have made every effort to preserve their marriages. Such persons seldom expect special treatment and often offer to take a lower profile in church activities for a while. Those who act as if nothing has happened and who demand to lead and serve without repentance and appropriate counsel pose a problem for the contemporary congregation. They fail to take into account what effect the divorce could have on the church's witness. Whatever the difficulties, Hi-C churches will deal thoughtfully and openly with the morality of divorce.

Morality is more than personal piety or even family piety. The suffering of children, adults in poverty, the aged, and those who are in political bondage are also moral issues. Most of the issues are complex and easy answers aggravate rather

> *Christians seem particularly susceptible to the error that grace is a license for sloppiness or piety a substitute for performance.*
> —R. C. Sproul (1991, 149)

O. C. Lewis looked upon his business as a tool to be employed in becoming directly involved in the Lord's work, and not only to provide for his family. A pivotol test of this attitude came in the early 1940s, when he faced twin agonies: the construction on the first church building was halted because of a lack of funds, and the business was facing bankruptcy for the third time during those difficult depression and war years. My father decided to mortgage our home but was torn between applying the money toward the business or toward the church. He later confessed to me that under any other circumstances he would have done the logical thing and applied it to the business, since a healthy business would aid the church. But this occasion was different, for he sensed it was a test of his priorities. After secluding himself for a half day in prayer and meditation, he made his decision. He called the workers to tell them to return to work on the church building—there would be money to pay them. By his own account the business immediately took a turn for the better, every year since, business has been better than the previous year.

Such experiences reinforced his conviction that God had given him the business to use for the advancement of His kingdom.
—David Lewis (1978, 10)

than solve problems. The Hi-C church avoids one-issue orientation while at the same time it quickens its membership to participate in solving critical human problems in the local and world communities. How else could it be a high commitment church were it not as concerned about these matters as was its Lord and Savior?

Leadership Is Special

Leadership is special in a high commitment church. Spiritual qualifications rather than marketplace skills are the first bases for selecting leaders; as described in Acts 6:3-4:

- persons in good standing   • wise
- full of the Spirit

Spiritual gifts rather than vacant organizational positions guide the placement of persons for ministry. Assigning leadership roles is not a means to get persons involved; results of such a plan can be devastating. Involvement is a prerequisite for leadership, not the other way around.

Pastoral and lay leaders are expected to be exemplary in life-style and in responsible stewardship, without exception. Pastors or lay leaders do err, make mistakes, and individually and collectively make poor judgments at times, but they are expected to be pacesetters in the life and ministry of the church.

Quality! Quality! Quality! Quality is the word that is used repeatedly by researchers to describe what people are expecting, even demanding, of churches. Not every congregation can do every type of ministry well. That is not the issue. The issue: persons looking for a church will not long tolerate pastors and congregations that do whatever they do poorly. Hi-C churches demand of themselves quality ministry in every area of service they undertake. A Hi-C church gives attention to doing all things well.

Spirituality

Spirituality is openly discussed, sought and encouraged in a higher commitment church. Spirituality is not viewed as something separate from and unrelated to personal, family,

Consider the Meridian, Mississippi, pastor and church that the Wall Street Journal reported on recently. In 1977, ninety six percent of this three hundred-member black congregation was on welfare. The concerned pastor called the members together to help them see that they had the buying power to deliver themselves—providing they spent their money right. As a result, church members combined their food stamps, purchased items from a wholesale grocer, and began operating a store out of the church auditorium.

In just four months the members earned enough money to purchase a supermarket. Today, the church owns a four thousand-acre farm, seven tractors, hundreds of cattle, two meat-packing plants, a bakery, three restaurants, and an auto repair shop. And none of its members are on welfare, because they are employed by the church.

Needless to say, the economic empowerment they experienced put member families in better positions to support their church.

Pastor Ronald Fowler (Akron, Ohio) believes the church has failed a parishioner who is still on welfare after a year of membership at Arlington Church. Bishop Luke Edwards (the Meridian, Mississippi, pastor) says it is his responsibility— not the government's—to wean his congregation off welfare. Preach deliverance to welfare captives!

—Sethard A. Beverly (1993, 5)

and community life; spirituality finds expression in all of these relationships. Spirituality is a dimension of life that is not attainable through human educational and economic processes.

Spirituality witnesses to a daily walk with God and an awareness of God's involvement in one's life. Spirituality is discovery and practice, however falteringly, of disciplines of meditation, confession, and praise. Spirituality is a commitment to see persons and events in light of God's purpose and sovereignty. Spirituality is a commitment to the mind of Christ.

Hi-C churches pray together about their mutual concerns and the problems of the world. Hi-C churches do not hesitate to let their prayer expressions outrun their theologies of prayer, knowing full well that the Holy Spirit interprets and intercedes.

Hi-C churches operate on the basis that the purposes and vision of the church are not always consistent with the ways and means of common business practice. Faith in what will happen is not an excuse for foolish expenditures but it is a confidence in more than what is obvious to the unconverted.

Hi-C churches suggest ways and tools for members to develop spirituality. They rely on the insights of persons who pray, who are visionary, and who are optimistic about the future of the church.

Hi-C churches are spiritual communities and, whatever else they appropriately might be, the high commitment church is a group of persons committed to the idea that they are in fact the body of Christ.

FOR MEDITATION OR DISCUSSION

1. Which way do you tend to lean in your thinking?
   __ The church has to be very specific in its demands on members.
   __ The church needs to be very broad in its standard for membership.
   __ The church needs to state its standards clearly but be hesitant to make demands on members to live up to the standard.
   __ The church needs to trust Christians to develop their own standards and be accepting of all who claim Christ.
   __ Other:

2. Name two of the mission efforts in which your congregation is involved in the local community. In the world.
   •

   •

3. Is your congregation a high-commitment church? Why did you answer as you did?

4. What practical guides should a local congregation have in regard to divorce? Sexual intercourse outside of marriage? Dishonesty in business affairs? Lying or cheating? Abuse in the family?

5. What are some of the reasons high-commitment churches are more likely to grow?

6. In what ways does your congregation recognize that leadership is special? Pastoral leadership? Lay leadership?

7. Do the members of your family easily converse about spiritual matters? If so, what subjects arise most often?

Do any of your friendship or work groups easily discuss spiritual matters?

Do members of your church easily discuss spiritual matters?

In what church groups do you feel most free to discuss your own spiritual life, or that of your family?

8. What is it about your church that makes it an enriching fellowship and a vital witness for Christ in your community? Or, what steps would your local church need to take to become the vibrant church you would like for it to be and the kind of church your community needs?

9

Joy

Joy is the asterisk of the Christian faith.
Joy is a witness to our hope in Christ.

JOYFUL JACQUELINE

The face of Jacqueline Basha comes to mind when I think about a joyful Christian. On January 15, 1979 in Theopolis, Lebanon I requested she take a few minutes from her work schedule at an orphanage run by her and her husband George. She was slender, kind, and often smiling even though she cared for seven of her own children and twenty-one others whose parents had been killed in the war. Jacqueline's and George's home had been an orphanage for nearly ten years. As we conversed, I asked, "Who helps you with the work?"

Jacqueline answered, "I do the work myself. I cook, wash clean, teach (help with homework), and change the babies' clothes." Her day began at 5:45 A.M. and ended at "ten, or eleven, or twelve—whenever I finish my work." I had watched her work and knew that she also mixed concrete and carried heavy bags of cement. She was eager to see the construction completed on the new facilities for the orphanage.

The children called her auntie and shared their problems with her. I observed, "You seem to love them all."

> *The Kingdom of God with all its joyful celebration is still in the future. It will not fully come until a certain trumpet is sounded to herald the return of the Lord of the party, who then will reside over the festivities as the ultimate Master of Ceremonies. But what is to come is to be enjoyed now in part.*
>
> *Whenever Christians party, they provide a foretaste of what is to come. Whenever they celebrate with laughter and song, they evangelize. They send out the message that the Kingdom of God is at hand—and the Kingdom of God is a wonderful party.*
> —Tony Campola (1990, 30)

"Yes," she said, "all of them. I hug them all—every day. And kiss them every day, too. And we play together. And we sometimes work together as we did when we needed the gravel on our entry road."

I suggested that she must get very tired. Smiling, she insisted, "No, I don't get tired. Or, if I sometimes do, God helps me." She concluded, "I feel that I do not live an empty life. My days have been full." Jacqueline enjoyed her vocation as a mother to nearly thirty children.

I do not suggest by Jacqueline's story that one needs to be exhausted at the end of the day or deprived of some of the simple privileges of life in order to have joy. We learn from her, however, that one can find joy even in the most demanding circumstances of life.

In the American culture especially, and perhaps in many other cultures, we often relate the presence of joy to increased wealth. In reality, material wealth and joy have no essential relationship. We can identify with the fellow who said, "I'd rather be rich," but, of course, rich people are not necessarily joyful people and many people who are poor by worldly standards have a contagious joy in very difficult circumstances.

ROBIN AND PURNIMA

Robin Das and his wife Purnima invited me and my fellow travelers to their home for refreshments. We had met this well-educated and committed couple in the United States and conversed often with them. Their Bangladesh home was quite humble. Appliances we consider essential in American homes were not present; stoves and other equipment were primitive by comparison. The house was inviting but not a match for even minimal houses in the neighborhoods where we lived in the United States. Yet we felt a warmth in the home. They smiled graciously and were cordial hosts. They communicated joy in the work they were doing, though both had known what it is to suffer for the cause of Christ. It was obvious they knew how to have fun and rejoice in circumstances that might have disheartened those of us who were their guests.

The opposite has been true in some households I have visited. More than a few times I have been with families who had every conceivable convenience and luxury items in every room of their houses, but the homes were sad ones. In some cases bitterness was expressed often; in others, skepticism about people and things was on the lips of adults and children. Money did not bring joy.

This lack of joy may be evident in another way. We were having dinner with very dear Christian friends. They said, "Before we can relax and have any fun together, even carry on a conversation, we have to get out of town. So, we take a trip together as often as possible." We commend them for recognizing their problem, in part, and for discovering a way to have refreshing times together. It is amazing, however, that they have a dream house to live in, considerable satisfaction in their vocations, and all the comforts that money can buy. Yet, they have to leave town to have memorable, joyous experiences; life is too busy and complicated at home.

Though sufficient wealth for life's necessities is desirable, money does not guarantee joy. Even some who live on a poverty level express a deep joy in life that is obviously not explained by their material circumstances.

> *Years ago ... I was taught that the name Isaac (Yishaq in Hebrew) means laughter . . . . When Sarah was told she would be pregnant, she laughed in disbelief. But God had the last laugh. A son was born to them in their old age and the mirthless human laugh turned into the Father's laughter of love. "They named their son 'Laughter' (Isaac) for he was a sign of the triumph of God's levity over man's gravity."*
> —Brennan Manning (157-158)

JOYS OF THE CHRISTIAN

What is this unique joy we talk about in relation to our Christian faith? Christian joy is experienced in a variety of ways. We will consider the following:

joy of inner assurance
joy of praise
joy of fun, even hilarity
joy of shared stories
joy of being together

Joy of Assurance

The joy of inner assurance has at least two aspects that can repeatedly be meaningful in the life of the believer. The first one is *comfort* in time of distress. Many Christians have reminded themselves of God's faithfulness by quoting a promise originally made to Joshua: "I will never leave you or forsake you," augmented by the affirmation from Psalm 118, "The Lord is my helper; I will not be afraid. What can anyone do to me?" (Hebrews 12:5b and 6b).

The second joy of inner assurance is *confidence* in the face of a major problem or a difficult challenge. A theme verse for tough times and hard tasks is, "I can do all things through him who strengthens me" (Philippians 4:13).

Barbara Hughes tells of a different experience that she and her husband had that included a questioning of his vocation. They both had doubts about their faith. She said she "felt alone and afraid. I needed reassurance." Barbara turned to the scriptures and a "soaring, dancing excitement ... swept over me as I read ... 'Though he fall, he shall not be utterly cast down: for the Lord upholdeth him with his hand.'" She noticed this verse followed "The steps of a man are established by the Lord; and He delights in his way" (Psalm 37:23-24 NAS) (1987, 25).

Orel Hershiser, Los Angeles Dodgers baseball pitcher and 1988 Major League Player of the Year, speaks of a unique assurance and confidence that comes to him during a game. NBC's Bob Costas asked him about times he observed Hershiser sitting in the dugout with his head back and eyes closed. Orel, who speaks openly about his Christian commitment and convictions, answered:

"I was singing hymns to myself to relax and keep my adrenaline down, because every time I thought about being ahead, I got too excited to pitch."

"How can you be so composed after a season like this and a playoff and World Series performance like this that has, it's fair to say, etched you a spot eternally in baseball lore?"

"Well, I feel that the Lord has blessed me with composure and has kept me calm through the whole thing. I know this isn't a religious show, but I just thank God for everything that's happened this year for our ball club" (1989, 206).

Inner assurance buttressed by the scriptures is "joy unspeakable" as the hymn says, in the worst or the best of times.

Joy of Praise

Following a recent worship service a member of our church remarked, "I felt a tingle inside me when we concluded the service. Ken Gill, the associate pastor, had preached an excellent sermon on renewal. At the end of the sermon he invited us, several hundred, to join hands as we stood in the aisles around the sanctuary. Sandi Patti sang and it was a time of praise, commitment, and renewal for many." No wonder the man felt a tingle. It is a *joy to praise the Lord.*

Praise in the company of other Christians does not always need to result in a physical sensation. Should it not happen often? Many persons experience moments of praise in only solemn moods and participate in worship services out of a sense of duty. A desirable quality is missing when the senses are not often involved in the celebration of God's presence.

Music is one way we worship with a variety of experiences. My worship is magnificently expressed as I listen to a choir sing Brahms "How Lovely Is Thy Dwelling Place." My chest feels full, I am involved both physically and spiritually in the praise, even though I am totally quiet. My friend Robert Nicholson would appreciate that anthem but has often said his favorite expression of praise is the hymn "Great Is Thy Faithfulness." Bedford Robinson, Sr., a retired pastor who was a member of a church I pastored in Sikeston, Missouri, was deeply moved when the choir sang a simple gospel song, "Neither Do I Condemn Thee."

Praise is a joyful experience and joy can be a part of the weekly celebrations of both small and large congregations. Perhaps it can not happen every week, but a *tingle* inside a worshiper is appropriate and desirable.

Joy of Fun

The joy of fun and hilarity is often lost in a preoccupation with serious matters, both for individual Christians and for local congregations. The weightiness of human sin persistently comes to the mind of the Christian. A burden of concern for the church's mission occupies the thinking of individuals and Christian groups. Prayer life is often focused on the desperate needs of the world, family, and friends. We are called to take up a cross and follow Jesus. Fun and hilarious times of laughter may seem incongruous with the weighty realities and may be left out of an individual's or a congregation's life for months. In the context of present world conditions, fun and hilarity can be thought inappropriate.

Since my youth I have not let studies or work keep me from conversing with friends and enjoying a good laugh. Later in life, at a time when I was very discouraged with my pastoral leadership and the state of the church, my wife observed, "Oral, it has been a long time since I have heard you laugh." Of all the major subjects we discussed that day, and the decisions we made, that remark is the one that remains with me. I remember I felt a desperate hunger for a good laugh.

Fun and hilarity are a part of the Christian life. Though desperation and despair are a part of life, we miss an essential ingredient when we do not have laughter. The church is richer when abandonment in laughter is often a part of the fellowship.

We have fun in our church. Recently our women's organization sponsored a fellowship supper. They were able to persuade our dignified pastoral staff, five persons, to dress as a motorcycle gang and do a lip-sync of a popular song. It was hilarious and enriching to the life of the church. Jesus loved it, I have no doubt.

We have fun in our family. Our family traveled with me one summer as I made contact with church groups throughout the western part of the United States. All six of us crowded into the Chevrolet and pulled behind us a pop-up camper. We recall with pleasure times of great fun. Once, high in the Rockies, somewhere in Montana, I challenged my twelve-year old son Doug, "If you will walk across that stream of ice-cold water, I will give you a Snickers candy bar." Ignoring his mother's protest, he began the walk. His feet were numb half-way across so he fell to his stomach and proceeded to crawl the distance. Then he had to come back. He laughed, we laughed, and his mother has started to laugh with the thirty-fifth retelling of the story. It was a hilarious time for a Christian family. I produced the Snickers and his mother dug out fresh warm clothes from the pop-up trailer. Fun is a valuable part of life, and a wonderful memory.

All kinds of groups, not just churches, can have fun times. All families, not just Christian families, can have fun times. Our culture too often associates fun with cruises, theme parks, and other experiences that require spending enormous amounts of money. The Christian, the Christian family, and the church can
- demonstrate fun in the common experiences of life
- affirm that fun is a part of the abundant life in Christ
- enjoy and use fun as a winsome aspect of the faith.

Joy of Shared Stories
Wanda dropped by my office to let me know that she and her husband Eddie were going to Egypt to serve with our missionaries for a year. Wanda's story is a familiar one to me, for she and I were in high school together and in the same church youth group. This was just another interesting episode in our shared stories of worship, fun, fellowship, and all the other rich experiences that are a part of our Christian faith.

Wanda and I both would be pleased to sit and listen to another story and enjoy it for the twentieth or thirtieth time. It is the story of how Hillery and Pauline Rice were converted.

Rejoice in the Lord always; again I will say, Rejoice. Let your gentleness be known to everyone. The Lord is near. Do not worry about anything, but in everything by prayer and supplication with thanksgiving let your requests be made known to God. And the peace of God, which surpasses all understanding, will guard your hearts and your minds in Christ Jesus.
—Philippians 4:4-7

He was a very successful salesman in Tulsa in the late thirties. They lived well, dressing in fine clothes and driving snazzy automobiles. One evening they attended a revival service in a local church and when the preacher invited people to accept Christ the tall salesman took his pretty wife's hand and they went forward and accepted Christ. They soon felt the call to the pastoral ministry. He gave up his job and they began a sacrificial period of preparation for this new vocation. Hillery attended college and pastored a small congregation, and in a few years he and Pauline began a fruitful ministry, which was to touch thousands of lives.

The reason Wanda and I would enjoy the story again is because Hillery and Pauline were our pastors and instrumental in challenging both of us, and dozens of other young people, to enter a church related vocation. Hillery's and Pauline's story is a common treasured possession for many of us who serve in the church today in many parts of the world.

Another shared story that has brought joy to a multitude of persons comes to mind. It is about a dream fulfilled. Helen talked to her children when they were home for the Christmas holidays in 1967 and then wrote a letter to some friends in January 1968. She told them that the small church her husband Bill was pastoring did not have much possibility of growing with its present circumstances. She suggested that several families could make a joint commitment to grow a church in Casper, Wyoming, and invited them to move to the western city to help.

Not many persons responded but the ones who did made all the difference. Son Norm and his wife Marcia, school teachers, agreed to come. Daughter Marilyn and her husband Harry, a coach, agreed to move to Casper. Bill's brother Bob and wife Blanche came, also. Not much response, one might say. Norm, however, became a gifted worship leader and was an incurable optimist. Harry and Marilyn became exemplary and energetic youth leaders. Bob, aided by Blanche, was a superb greeter, learning children's names from the first time he met them. The church began to grow and soon called a full-time pastor. Property was purchased and a first-unit

> *Far and away the most important benefit of celebration is that it saves us from taking ourselves too seriously. It is an occupational hazard of devout folk to become stuffy bores. That should not be. Of all people we should be the most free, alive, interesting. Celebration adds a note of gaiety, festivity, hilarity to our lives. After all, Jesus rejoiced so fully in life that He was accused of being a wine-bibber and a glutton. Many of us lead such sour lives that we couldn't possibly be accused of such things.*
>
> *... I am suggesting that we do need deeper, more earthy experiences of exhilaration. It is healing and refreshing to cultivate a wide appreciation for life ... Celebration helps us to relax and enjoy the good things of the earth.*
>
> —Richard J. Foster (1978, 168)

worhip center/gymnasium was built. It was soon crowded, with an average of more than 125 persons each Sunday. A sanctuary seating almost three hundred was built that would serve the congregation for years to come. Within three years the congregation was having duplicate Sunday morning worship services. Eventually a retail store with a large warehouse was purchased and remodeled into a church facility of seventy thousand square feet, including a beautiful, large sanctuary. The congregation now numbers about eight hundred each Sunday morning.

That is Helen's story. It all became possible because a fantastic vision was followed with a letter in 1968. That letter lies on my desk as I repeat the story for you.

In the fellowship of Christians some stories are heavy with meaning and others are humorous. I love to hear Dr. Forrest Robinson, president of Mid-America Bible College, tell of a baptism service in the Jackson, Mississippi, church he pastored. The congregation occupied a new facility and a baptismal pool was not a part of the first unit. He decided to build a plywood structure and line it with fiberglass. On the day of the baptism the temporary pool was filled with water, the candidates were ready, and a large congregation present. Pastor Robinson stepped into the pool and was joined by a man who was to be baptized. As the man was immersed the front side of the pool broke loose and water poured out onto the congregation. Those on the front rows gained some idea of how the Egyptian soldiers pursuing the Israelites felt when the Red Sea came rushing in upon them.

Shared stories of difficult times, of victories, of humorous events, of personal experiences, and of group experiences are a great joy. Everyone in your church, and everyone in my church has a wonderful story that needs to be shared.

Joy of Being Together

Jack, a single young man, had been a Christian for only a few years. We had just finished working together on a church remodeling project and were having a Coke together. He said, "You know, I begin to long for church on Thursday. Out in the oil fields the language is coarse and the stories are, at best, dirty. People cheat each other out of money and oil rights, and employees loaf when a boss is not there to watch them. It used not to bother me but since I accepted Christ that type of thing gets me down. Church lifts me up. Just to be in a decent conversation and talk about things that really matter makes me come alive."

Suzan explained to her youth minister that the most fun she ever had was at church on Sunday and in youth fellowship on Wednesday evening. She explained, "I get the feeling that I really matter to someone when I am here." The youth minister listened without comment for he knew Suzan's home was often far from happy. Church was an oasis for Suzan.

Mildred told her small group that she had at first decided not to come for the weekly meeting but had changed her mind. Tonight, she said, she had to have their prayers and their hugs for "I learned this afternoon that I have cancer."

Judy says she goes to church "because that is what I have always done since I was a child and I would miss all the warm fellowship if I were not here as often as I can be."

A joy for the Christian is participation in the fellowship; just being present with other Christians. Some shake hands, some give a simple greeting, some are huggers, some cry even over good experiences, some laugh whatever the circumstance, and some always have an encouraging word. Whatever and whomever, it is a joy for Christians to be together and "encourage one another and build up each other" (1 Thess. 5:11).

Joy is a part of the abundant life in Christ. The individual follower of Christ and local congregations can anticipate that joy will be a part of the Christian experience, even in the most demanding circumstances. The absence of joy may indicate a need to discover ways of letting joy happen.

It is easily forgotten that the fellowship [of Christians] is a gift of grace, a gift of the Kingdom of God that any day may be taken from us, that the time that still separates us from utter loneliness may be brief indeed. Therefore, let him who until now has had the privilege of living a common Christian life with other Christians praise God's grace from the bottom of his heart. Let him thank God on his knees and declare: It is grace, nothing but grace, that we are allowed to live in community with Christian [friends].
—Dietrich Bonhoeffer in Nazi Germany (1954, 20)

FOR MEDITATION OR DISCUSSION

1. Name a joyful person you know. How does he or she brighten your day?

2. Do you have a favorite scripture you quote when you have a problem or difficult situation?

   Do you have a scripture cr a saying you recall when you have a major challenge or are facing a demanding task?

3. Describe how you feel when you are having an unusually enjoyable experience of praise and worship.

   Name a hymn, anthem, or gospel song that expresses well your praise for God.

4. How long has it been since you had fun? What was the occasion? What is keeping you from having fun more often?

   What events or meeting with friends would you need to plan in order to have some fun soon?

What changes in your thinking would you have to make in order to enjoy life more?

5. Briefly recall or tell a story from some friend's life. Why is it encouraging, enlightening, or funny?

What is one of the best stories in the life of your family?

6. When you meet with people, what is your favorite way of greeting, affirming, and building other persons up? Do you
__ hug   __ shake hands
__ give a compliment __ relay a compliment
__ smile   __ converse
__ invite to dinner   __ ask advice
__ other:

7. In a sentence, how would you summarize your appreciation for the group with which you worship?

8. How do you bring joy to other Christians in your fellowship?

APPENDIX

(Guide and materials for thirteen weeks with
a small group or Sunday school class)

SESSION #1: INTRODUCTORY SESSION
Distribute book Hi-Q Christians and use the following questions and statements to guide discussion. These pages may be duplicated. See page 3 for suggestions on how to use in small groups and in Sunday school classes.

1. "It was in Antioch that the disciples were first called 'Christians,' " (Acts 11:26). Why, do you think, were the first-century followers of Jesus Christ called by this name? How were their lives different from other religious persons of their day?

2. It is rather easy to identify bad things that are happening in the world, the community, and the church, and perhaps it is best for us to face the reality of evil regularly. Today, however, our focus will be a positive one.
What are some good things that are happening
   • in the world?

   • in our community?

   • in our local church?

   • in your life?

3. If God appointed you the Vice-President for Improvements for the next five years, what change would you make
   • in the world?   • in the local church?
   • in the community?   • in your self?

4. How effective is your voice in bringing about change?

	effective	somewhat effective	not effective
• in the community	____	____	____
• in local church	____	____	____
• in your family	____	____	____
• in your self	____	____	____

If you and five other persons agree that change is in order in one of these areas, how effective would your united voice be?

5. What would need to happen for you to have renewal (or refreshment) in your Christian life?

___ a decision to seek renewal

___ confession

___ a renewal emphasis in my church

___ on my part, a more faithful practice of this Christian discipline: _____

___ an inner sense of forgiveness

___ forgiving someone else

___ someone to help me understand my needs

___ other:

6. As you consider the opportunities for your local church in your community over the next five years, are you optimistic, pessimistic, or realistic? Why?

SESSIONS 2-10

The discussion questions at the end of each chapter may serve as guides for each session. At the conclusion of each session, the leader will identify for the group the chapter that is to be read in preparation for the next meeting. It is not necessary, however, for everyone to read the material; the questions are worded so that even persons who have not read the chapter can enter into the discussion. Questions may be copied.

SESSION 11: GUEST CHRISTIAN

Invite an exemplary Christian to meet with your group. Give the guest the following instructions:

We would like for you to talk about your Christian experience, tell us how you have grown, identify some disciplines or times that have been difficult, and where you are now in your Christian journey.

The guest may want to look through the book you have been studying so as to be informed on the subjects you have been discussing.

You may prefer to interview a guest. An interview format enables the leader to guide the participation of the guest and the group. A set of four or five questions could be prepared in advance and the guest given a copy at least a day or two in advance of your meeting.

Another option: invite two or three exemplary Christians to meet with your group and briefly talk about their spiritual pilgrimages.

SESSION 12: PRAYER
(One Option)

Focus on prayer for renewal. "The prayer of the righteous is powerful and effective" (James 5:16). An outline possibility:

1. Read James 3:16 and other scriptures on prayer such as Luke 11:5-13.

2. The leader may briefly give examples of answered prayer for an individual or a church or ask for examples from others in the group.

3. List on a sheet of paper or a chalkboard prayer requests for your church and community, and for individuals in your group. Read list aloud after all the requests are listed.

4. Ask one person to be prepared to lead the group in prayer or, if members of your group pray extemporaneously, indicate that several persons may lead in prayer for any one or several of the listed requests.

5. Have available a commitment card or sheet that may read as follows:

I will pray this week for the following requests that were listed by my group:

Signed _____

Date _____

Encourage each person to list three requests for which they will be praying during the coming week. Encourage each to choose one request related to the life of the church.

SESSION 12: THE PASTOR
(A Second Option)

Invite the pastor of your church to meet with your group and talk about his or her vision for the church and the renewal the congregation needs to experience in order to realize that vision. The pastor may also be encouraged to talk about spiritual disciplines the pastor feels should be more prominent in the life of the members. Request that some time be left for questions and answers. The leader will want to be prepared with a few questions to start the discussion.

If the pastor is not available, a leading lay person or an associate pastor may meet with the group.

CONCLUDING SESSION: TOWARD RENEWAL

The group has been considering the need for high quality Christians and high commitment churches. Renewal is essential in every congregation—a new inspiration, new challenge, a renewed sense of the Spirit's leadership.

Develop with your group a one-year plan toward renewal for your local congregation.

What events will encourage renewal?

What classes need to be offered?

What challenges need to be stated to members?

What specific evangelism efforts need to be initiated?

Remind the group that it is easy to begin listing ideas and suggestions that were effective in former years but may no longer be as effective in many locations. Focus on present-day needs, schedules, problems, and opportunities as you develop a plan for renewal. Remember, also, the group is making suggestions and not decisions. A list of the suggestions, however, may be appreciated by the pastor.

Bibliography

Allen, Ronald and Gordon Borror. 1982. *Worship: Rediscovering the Missing Jewel.* Portland, Ore: Multnomah.

Anderson, Leith. 1992. *A Church for the Twenty-First Century.* Minneapolis: Bethany House Pub.

Anthony, Carl Sferrazza. 1993. "Hillary Clinton: What I Hope to Do as First Lady." *Good Housekeeping.* (Jan.): 98.

Applegarth, Margaret T. 1957. *Twelve Baskets Full.* New York: Harper and Brothers Pub.

Barna, George. 1990. *The Frog in the Kettle.* Ventura, Calif: GL Publications, Regal Books.

_____. 1991. *User Friendly Churches.* Ventura, Calif: GL Publications, Regal Books.

Beverly, Sethard A. 1993. *Metro-Voice.* Anderson, Ind: Board of Church Extension and Home Missions of the Church of God (special issue).

Bonhoeffer, Dietrich. 1954. *Life Together.* New York: Harper and Row, Pub.

Buechner, Frederick. 1982. *The Sacred Journey.* San Francisco: Harper and Row Pub.

Callen, Barry L. 1992. *She Came Preaching: The Life and Ministry of Lillie S. McCutcheon.* Anderson, Ind: Warner Press.

Campolo, Tony. 1990. *The Kingdom of God Is a Party.* Dallas: Word Pub.

Chafin, Kenneth. 1985. *The Communicator's Commentary* Vol. 7. Waco, Tex: Word Books.

Colson, Charles. 1992. *Christianity Today.* (Oct.5).

Cornell, George W. 1992. Anderson, Ind: *Anderson Herald Bulletin.* Associated Press. (Dec. 5).

Covey, Stephen R. 1989. *The Seven Habits of Highly Effective People.* New York: Simon and Schuster. A Fireside Book.

Doucette, Michael in Arterburn, Stephen and Jack Felton. 1991. *Toxic Faith.* Nashville: Oliver Nelson. A Division of Thomas Nelson Pub.

Dunwiddie, Fred. 1991. Report for an Anderson School of Theology class.

Foster, Richard J. 1978. *Celebration of Discipline.* New York: Harper and Row Pub.

Gaither, Gloria. 1988. *We Have This Moment.* Waco, Tex: Word Books.

Gallup, George, Jr. 1991. *National and International Religion Report* (May 20).

George, Carl F. 1991. *Prepare Your Church for the Future.* Tarrytown, N.Y: Fleming H. Revell Co.

Graham, Ruth Bell. 1982. *It's My Turn.* Old Tappan, NJ: Fleming H. Revell Co.

Hershiser, Orel with Jerry B. Jenkins. 1989. *Out of the Blue.* Brentwood, Tenn: Wolgemuth and Hyatt Pub.

Hesteness, Roberta. 1988. *Leadership* (Fall): 15.

Huffman, John. 1991. In a symposium "The Power and the Presence." *Leadership* (Summer).

Hughes, Kent and Barbara. 1987. *Liberating Ministry from the Success Syndrome.* Wheaton, Ill: Tyndale House Pub.

Hughes, R. Ken. 1992. *Disciplines of a Godly Man.* As quoted in *Christianity Today* (May 18).

Kelley, Dean. 1986. *Why Conservative Churches Are Growing.* Macon, Ga: Mercer University Press. Rose edition.

Kelly, Thomas R. n.d. *A Testament of Devotion.* New York: Harper and Brothers.

Kimball, Roger. 1992. *New Criterion.* As quoted in Context 24 (Nov.) no. 19 of *The Selected Letters of Bertrand Russell.* Vol. 1. New York: Houghton Mifflin.

Lewis, David. 1978. *Vital Christianity.* (Jan. 15): 10.

MacDonald, Gail. 1989. *Keep Climbing.* Wheaton, Ill: Tyndale.

Manning, Brennan. 1986. *Lion and Lamb.* Old Tappan, NJ: Fleming H. Revell Co.

McCartney, Bill with Dave Diles. 1990. *From Ashes to Glory.* Nashville: Thomas Nelson Pub.

Nevitt, JoRene. 1991-2. Anderson, Ind: *The Clergy Wives' Newsletter.* n.p. (Winter).

Nouwen, Henri J. M. 1976. *The Genesee Diary.* New York: Doubleday, an Image Book.

_____. 1981. *Making All Things New.* San Francisco: Harper and Row Pub.

Packer, J. I. 1991. In a Symposium "The Power and the Presence." *Leadership* (Summer).

Rather, Dan with Peter Wyden. 1991. *I Remember*. Boston: Little, Brown and Co.

Sproul, R. D. 1991. *The Hunger for Significance*. Ventura, Calif: GL Publications, Regal Books.

Stafford, Tim. 1992. "Ron Sider's Unsettling Crusade." *Christianity Today* (April 27): 18-22.

Stokes, Kenneth. 1990. *Faith Is a Verb*. Mystic, Conn: Twenty-Third Publications.

Swindoll, Charles R. 1982. *Strenthening Your Grip*. Waco, Tex: Word Books Pub.

Templeton, John Marks with James Ellison. 1987. *The Templeton Plan: Twenty-One Steps to Success and Happiness*. San Francisco: Harper and Row Pub.

Webster's New Twentieth Century Dictionary of the English Language, Unabridged. 1979. (No city given.) William Collins Pub.

Welch, Reuben. 1982. *We Really Do Need Each Other*. Nashville: Impact Books.